About the Author

Paul A. Kienel is executive director of the fast-growing California Association of Christian Schools. He earned B.A. degrees in theology and social science at Bethany Bible College and LaVerne College, respectively. He studied further at California State College, earning general elementary teaching credentials and doing graduate work equivalent to nearly two M.A. degrees. Azusa Pacific College conferred on him an honorary doctorate of humanities in 1972.

Dr. Kienel has served as an associate pastor, and later as a teacher and principal of Westminster Christian School, Westminster, Calif.

In his work for CACS, Dr. Kienel is a popular speaker at Christian school functions and on Christian college campuses. He counsels up to 70 groups a year who are planning new schools. He is writer and publisher of *Christian School Comment,* the official organ of CACS, and moderator of the daily radio program "Christian School Comment," on eight radio stations in California.

Dr. Kienel resides in Whittier, is married, and has three daughters.

THE
CHRISTIAN
SCHOOL:

Why It Is Right
for
Your Child

Paul A. Kienel

VICTOR BOOKS
a division of SP Publications, Inc.
WHEATON ILLINOIS 60187

Offices also in Fullerton, California • Whitby, Ontario, Canada • Amersham-on-the-Hill, Bucks, England

Seventh printing, 1980

Scripture quotations in this book credited NASB are from the
New American Standard Bible, © The Lockman Foundation,
La Habra, Calif., 1960, 1962, 1963, 1968, 1971, 1972, 1973;
other Bible quotations are from the King James Version.

Library of Congress Catalog Card Number: 74-77320
ISBN: 0-88207-703-1

VICTOR BOOKS
A division of SP Publications, Inc.
1825 College Avenue • Wheaton, Ill. 60187

Dedicated to
the ladies in my household:
my wife Annie
and my daughters
Sandi
Colleen
Cheryl

Contents

Foreword

For a hundred years the Protestant church and public education in the United States were intertwined and, most of us assumed, inseparable.

The Lord's Prayer and the Golden Rule were taught in most every schoolroom every day. Traditional Christian religious holidays were observed in classrooms, school assemblies, and extracurricular school programs.

Since the Supreme Court banned prescribed prayers from public schools, there has been a national revival of interest in private schools.

Also, grotesque misbehavior, individual and organized, which now characterizes many public schools has alienated both *students and faculty*.

Private church-related schools heretofore could not compete in the open market against the higher teachers' salaries available in tax-subsidized schools. Now many teachers, some fearing for their personal safety, flee the blackboard jungle for the happier environment of a "selective" school. If there is less pay, there are more "fringe benefits" on a Christian campus.

Years ago it was argued that students maturing in a "sheltered environment" would, like hothouse plants, be unprepared for the cold outside world.

Now more and more Americans are realizing that it is in fact the public or state-school student who is "overprotected." He is "sheltered" from religious instruction and exposed to all forms of non-Christian philosophy and behavior.

Dr. Kienel explains the forces behind the resurgence of the Christian school movement. But perhaps more significant than anything else is the fact that Americans know they now need an educational program that goes beyond the "do your own thing" philosophy of the sick '60s. Parents seeking out Christian schools for their youngsters are looking for a learning environment that is more disciplined, that promotes patriotism, and where the Bible is not the most dreaded book of the classroom. Christian schools are coming into their own at a time when the truth they represent may very well be the only hope for the next generation.

PAUL HARVEY
ABC NEWS Commentator

Preface

For the past several years I have written a monthly one-page flier called *Christian School Comment* for the California Association of Christian Schools. A sample copy of each issue has been sent to more than 1,000 Christian schools around the country. The monthly circulation has steadily increased with some issues selling as high as 40,000 copies. The topics covered in *Christian School Comment* over the years were the starting point for several chapters of this book.

I am hopeful the message on the pages that follow will cause many parents to seek out the advantages of Christian school education for their children. The present-day phenomenon of the Christian school explosion is, in my judgment, one of the great untold stories of our time. It is an inspiring story because Christ is at the center. Christians are learning that there is a compatible relationship between Christ and education. Jesus said, "I am . . . the Truth," and imparting truth is the very heart of education All truth, be it science, math, history, or philosophy is inseparably related to Christ and the Bible. Therefore, Christians of all people, should be deeply involved in education and in a program of education that holds Christ forth in His rightful place.

I am very much aware that I have included some strongly worded statements—negative statements if you will. Some persons will not agree with them though most are made by responsible spokesmen in their respective fields. All will recognize, however, that a trend toward the development of Christian schools is very much a part of today's scene. This book is intended to help spread that word and give background to some of the forces behind it.

I owe a special debt of gratitude to Phil Landrum of Wheaton, Illinois, who assisted me with the manuscript; to Laurie McGuyre, my able secretary, who typed and edited my copy; and to my wife and three daughters who put up with my wide expanse of papers, pamphlets, and books in their precious sewing room for weeks on end while I finished this project. I am also indebted to my gracious staff of 10 tremendous people who have carried part of my work load while I hammered out the manuscript.

PAUL A. KIENEL

P. O. Box 4097
Whittier, Calif. 90607

The surging Christian school movement represents a new current, a new direction in the Bible-believing church world.

1

The Christian
School Explosion

Maybe you've heard of the new mother, typically proud and excited about her newborn daughter. I don't know her name, nor her hometown, just her unusual story. Almost immediately after coming home from the hospital, she and her husband enrolled their daughter in the kindergarten of a nearby Christian school. Five years in advance!

"There's only one kind of education as far as I'm concerned," the young mother explained. "And that's a *Christian* school education. I want to make sure there is a place for my child when it comes time to send her to school."

Unusual? Yes, of course her actions are unusual, but not her thinking. It is consistent with an unprecedented nationwide interest on the part of many parents that is causing the Christian school movement literally to explode across the country. Consider these items about other parents and schools:

■ In Wheaton, Ill. nine parents formed their own car pool to travel a 20-mile round trip each day so their children could attend a Christian school. This expense, of course, is in addition to the monthly tuition for each child. Other parents are traveling even greater distances each day to send their children to Christian schools.

■ In Santa Ana, Calif. 65 students with their parents were turned away after they had waited their turn to enroll in Maranatha Christian Academy. Principal Neal Pirolo said, "This is our first year of operation and we simply could not go beyond our maximum of 400 students." He added, "We are providing for additional classes as rapidly as we can."

■ Pensacola (Florida) Christian School is the largest Christian school in America, having reached an enrollment of more than 3,000 students. Plans call for even more expansion, including opening a Christian college in the fall of 1974.

■ From 1965 to 1973 the California Association of Christian Schools increased from 68 to 350 member schools. The association's student population during that period mushroomed from 11,388 to 46,032. Other Christian school organizations around the country reflect similar patterns of growth.

Paradoxically, the Christian school movement is exploding at a time when other segments of private education are recording a decline. Catholic schools are currently losing six percent of their enrollment annually. They closed 365 schools in 1971. Military academies, popular in the '20s and '30s, are very much in decline. The elite private schools are barely holding their own in some areas and are diminishing in others.

Public schools in certain areas are also losing ground. The *Los Angeles Herald Examiner* quoted Dr. Wilson Riles, California state superintendent of public instruction, as saying in 1973 that there were "50,000 fewer students in California public schools this year than last." The Whittier, Calif., area school districts planned to close three public schools. Nearby Norwalk closed four public schools. A few miles east, the San Bernardino School District is in the process of selling five public school campuses. It is interesting to note that some of the Christian schools in the area are negotiating to purchase these former public school facilities. The declining birth rate accounts for a significant part of the public schools' enrollment decline, but that is not the complete answer.

U.S. News and World Report and *Christian Life* magazines published articles in 1973 about the burgeoning Christian school movement, referring to this phenomenon as the "Boom in Protestant Schools" and "The Christian School Explosion." According to *U.S. News,* this rapid rise of Protestant Christian schools is literally shaking the teeth of the government's public school establishment. Christ-centered Christian schools now represent the fastest growing educational movement in America. It is also one of the fastest growing segments of the Bible-believing church world.

What is behind it all? There is a "prairie fire" sense of urgency among many parents to find schools for their children that will not be at cross purposes with the teachings of the home and the church. Christian parents and church leaders alike are becoming weary of trying to compete with public schools for the minds of their children and young people.

A seventh-grade public school teacher who sends his son to a Christian school said of his experiences: "As I observe the operations of the public school, I notice that parents and teachers are much of the time at opposite poles of opinion about life, morals, and/or philosophy. I want my son to get the same information about life from school as he gets from home. I can *trust* the Christian school to get biblical principles over to him as a normal part of growing up. I do not have to 'undo' anything when he gets home."

With all of its problems, public education continues to hold a place of high esteem in the minds of many Americans. For decades, we have held public school education on the same high level as motherhood, apple pie, and the American flag. Multiplied thousands of wonderful people serve as teachers, administrators, and board members in the public school system. Many of these are dedicated Christians. Our Christian college movement in America has supported the public school teaching profession more than any other secular profession. The largest single department in most Christian colleges is the education department. As a result, there are probably more Christians per capita in public education than in any other secular field. This has been the established pattern for at least a quarter of a century.

Today, however, we see a gradual turning from this established pattern. In the early '70s no Christian college or university in America offered a master's degree in Christian School administration. Now several leading Christian colleges and at least one Christian university offer such a program.

Other Christian colleges have Christian school administration graduate programs in the planning stage. More and more future teachers in Christian colleges are being challenged to consider the Christian school ministry, and courses are being offered in the Christian philosophy of education. Pastors who never supported Christian schools before are beginning to promote local Christian schools or are establishing their own. One national Christian school association received a thousand inquiries last year on how to establish Christian schools. The Rev. Paul B. Smith, pastor of People's Church of Toronto, a church that gives more than a million dollars to missions each year, said in *Child Evangelism* magazine in 1971:

"If I had my life as a father to live over again, I would make whatever financial sacrifices would be necessary in order to send each of my children to a biblically centered school from kindergarten to the end of college.

"If I had my life as a pastor to live over again, I would warn my people constantly about the dangers of the North American public school system. Over a period of 30 years I have watched with a heavy heart the devastating effects of the public schools, both on my own children and those on many of my congregation."

Pastor Smith has established a Christian school in his church.

Parents by the thousands, a high percentage of them Christians, have now opted for a Christian school education for their children. Christians who at one time believed that they somehow had a religious obligation to use their children to neutralize or "save" the public school are now more concerned with the outcome of their own children than they are with the outcome of a given local public school system.

The surging Christian school movement represents

a new current, a new direction in the Bible-believing church world. There is a shifting of loyalties. There is an intense "grass roots" wave of parental concern for the preservation of children, a concern that will not be denied. The current trends indicate that the Christian school explosion has just begun.

The Christian school movement . . .
is flourishing today because
Christian schools are not limited to
a select parish, but are identified with
the Bible's "Great Commission,"
which commands Christians to
teach and preach the
truth to all people everywhere.

2

Are

Christian Schools

Parochial Schools?

When I was growing up in a small town in Oregon, a favorite pastime two of my buddies and I had was the "persecution" of kids from our town's parochial school. I assure you there was no love lost between the "public school" and the "private school" kids. The public school was out each day at 3 o'clock, while the parochial school dismissed at 3:30. This gave us time to race across town and begin our afternoon "sport."

We would hide in a field of tall grass near their school's bicycle rack. We'd wait until the students filed out of school and headed for their bikes —then it was target practice time. With youthful exuberance, we threw clumps of grass with wads of mud and roots still attached. We loved those moving targets and had no fear of retaliation because these parochial school kids had been taught not to react to persecution. This activity soon became our favorite form of after-school recreation. I regret now that I was such a rascal, but our boyish actions seemed to reflect the general disdain of Bible-believing Christians toward church-sponsored schools in the 1940s.

It wasn't until my college years that I heard about the rising Christian school movement among other groups of Christians. Because of my mud-slinging past with the parochial school kids, I had an immediate negative reaction. When I finally learned that there is a significant difference between the newer Christian schools and many of the older parochial schools, it greatly improved my level of enthusiasm.

Benjamin Disraeli, the colorful prime minister of Great Britain a century ago, said, "If you would converse with me, define your terms." Many people assume that a Christian school is a parochial school. Webster defines the word *parochial* as "confined or restricted as if within the borders of a parish." The new breed of Christian schools is not limited to the "borders of a parish" or to the constituents of a sponsoring church. These schools are Christ-centered, rather than church-centered—though most are sponsored by churches.

Aside from educating, the type of Christian school we're talking about does not generally indoctrinate youngsters toward a particular church or denomination, but seeks primarily to bring students into a right relationship with the Lord Jesus Christ. The decision of "which church" is left to the parents. Students from many denominational backgrounds attend these Christian schools. In fact, some students are enrolled with little or no background in religious instruction. Such students are welcome provided the parents understand that Christ will be presented as Saviour and Lord and the Bible offered as the infallible point of reference for making right decisions. In addition, Christian schools expect parents to support in the home what is taught in the classroom.

If the youngsters have already received Christ, then the Christian schools' primary mission is to offer Christian training as an extension of the home, and the church.

A strictly parochial school is a school sponsored by a church for the families of the sponsoring church or of that denomination. Their schools are established primarily to educate the young of their own church or parish, and generally to bring their students into membership of the sponsoring church.

Because most students in these schools are of one faith, they seldom encounter students of other faiths. They often see the same youngsters in church whom they see all week long. Such an environment has rightly been characterized as a "sheltered" or "cloistered" educational environment.

A major criterion for entrance into a Christian school is that the student be academically capable of the Christian school curriculum and that he work acceptably with others. Most Christian schools require basic entrance exams to determine these qualities and use standardized tests to evaluate their academic program. Socially, students who enroll in Christian schools must be willing to live and work by the rules of the school. Attendance at a private Christian school is a privilege, not a right.

As much as Christian schools would like to help, they are often not equipped to handle students with "severe" academic problems. However, more and more Christian schools are developing specialized programs for students with "slow-learner" problems. It is heart-warming to see what is being accomplished in this area.

The overall purpose of a Christian school is to provide a means by which a child can be inspired to live the Christian life in a non-Christian world. Christian schools are an effort to bring back a normal, Christian, disciplined educational environment for our youngsters. It is increasingly evident that the idea of a "nonparochial" Christian school is very much alive and doing well. The Christian school movement presented in this book is flourishing today because Christian schools are not limited to a select parish, but are identified with the Bible's "Great Comission," which commands Christians to teach and preach the *truth* to all people everywhere.

"There is—for the first time in
our history—an active loss
of enchantment with our schools."
Dr. Sidney P. Marland

3

Americans
Are Losing Faith

An ever-widening circle of the American public is questioning the trend of public education.

Dr. Sidney P. Marland, Jr., assistant secretary for education, U.S. Department of Health, Education, and Welfare, sums up the current public attitude toward education in the *U.S. News and World Report* article (Oct. 8, 1973) on the Christian school movement:

"There is manifest in the country—to my knowledge, for the first time in our history—an active loss of enchantment with our schools . . . from kindergarten through graduate school. For the first time, Americans in significant numbers are questioning the purpose of education, the competence of educators, and the usefulness of the system in preparing young minds for life in these turbulent times."

The U.S. Congressional Record of October 2, 1973 records the testimony of U.S. Congressman Earl Landgrebe (R., Ind.). He said, "Mr. Speaker, probably nothing has fallen from public favor more in recent years than public education. Widespread disillusionment is evident among parents and taxpayers over the billions they have lavished on U.S. education in recent times. In 1965, almost 80 percent of school bond referendums for public schools won approval; by 1972, the figure had dropped to 47 percent."

A national news analyst reported the results of a poll taken in 1972 that showed 31 percent of the American people thought well of the public schools compared with 61 percent in 1966. Americans generally are losing faith in a school system that was once considered by some to be the greatest school system in the world. A 1969 Gallup Poll revealed that "65 percent of those questioned felt private schools were equal or superior in quality to public schools." (Most Christian schools range from 3 to 18 months ahead of the national achievement test norm.) Even more astonishing, "59 percent asserted that they would send their children to nonpublic schools if tuition were free."

Many Americans outside the conservative church community are losing faith in the public school system for a variety of reasons.

Moral Depravity

Recent issues of the *San Francisco Chronicle* document the following: "Constitutional Law classes at Berkeley High School were the setting for student viewing of explicit, no-holds-barred, pornographic films. The subject matter was relevant to the obscenity issues that the classes were studying." Homosexuals have been invited to public junior high school classes in the San Francisco Bay area to share their "personal philosophy of life."

Drugs and Violence

Dr. Max Rafferty, in his book *Classroom Countdown* (Hawthorn), says, "In several of our big-city schools, policemen have to be stationed in the corridors in order to protect the teacher from his pupils, and the pupils from each other." Los Angeles is a typical example. The *Los Angeles Herald Examiner* reports, "The Los Angeles City Schools have recently appropriated $180,000 to hire 'safety aids' to patrol the halls, restrooms, and playgrounds of the Los Angeles City schools." The *American School Board Journal* reports that teaching school in some cities is already twice as dangerous as working in a steel mill!

A New York City pastor told me that already 50 percent of all the high school students and 30 percent of the elementary students in New York City are on drugs of some kind. He said that some of the girls from his church who attend the public schools are afraid to go into the girls restrooms the full day they are in school because of the potential violence there. "In order to support their drug habit," he said, "these youthful addicts have to acquire a rather substantial income every day. They have found that by holding up 'straight students' at knife point as they come into the restrooms, they can get the money they need."

Jack Hyles, whose church in Hammond, Ind. sponsors a complete kindergarten through college program, names the narcotics problem as one of the reasons his congregation was led to start its own schools.

Low Academics

Parents are disenchanted with government schools because of low academic standards in some of them. Dr. John R. Miles, writing in the new quarterly edition of the *Saturday Evening Post* (spring 1972), said:

"The nation's number one academic problem in education today is a reading problem. The U.S. Office of Education has estimated, 'There are 24 million people 18 years old or older in the United States who are functionally illiterate.

" 'That means they cannot read, write, or count well enough to handle the day-to-day tasks demanded of them in modern society; they cannot read well enough to know what bus to take to get to work, they cannot count the streets or read the street signs well enough to know when to get off the bus and transfer to another. Yet it isn't because they haven't gone to school. There are only 6.4 million Americans 14 years old and over who haven't gone through at least the fifth grade. So the inescapable conclusion is that the vast majority of those 24 million 'functionally illiterate' people went to school for at least five years but learned little except to hate school.' "

A Sunday edition of the *Los Angeles Herald Examiner* in 1972 editorialized that the state of California has now eliminated all specified academic requirements for high school graduation. Dr. Calvin Grieder, writing not long ago in *The Nation's Schools,* said:

"Relaxation of standards is apparent in so many aspects of life in these United States. In academic affairs I see this every day in the wide-spread abolition of grades, examinations, and attendance requirements."

High Cost

Many Americans are losing faith in their public schools because of the high cost of financing them. President Nixon is reported as saying in the spring 1973 *Saturday Evening Post,* "This nation is spending more money without corresponding results in education than any other country in history: some $60 to $70 billions a year goes into the public school systems—as much as the rest of the world together—and every year the school system turns out tens of thousands of high school graduates who can't read the diplomas they're handed."

California Governor Ronald Reagan said at the 1973 convention of the National Association of Secondary School Principals in Anaheim, Calif.: "In California, the total enrollment growth in grades kindergarten through 12 has been only 7.2 percent over the past six budget years. Yet, the state alone has increased its support for kindergarten through 12 by 45 percent in that same period." He added, "The public asks why more and more money is needed to educate fewer and fewer children."

Losing Control

Parents are losing faith in the public schools because they are generally losing control of them. In the last decade there has been a decline in public school boards throughout the country from 25,000 to 18,000. The October 10, 1973 edition of the *Indianapolis News* quotes U.S. Congressman Earl Landgrebe as saying: "If we continue down the road of extending and increasing federal aid to education, total central control of education is inevitable. Sooner or later we will have a centralized, standardized, uniform national school system. Only a full-fledged Communist or Fascist would advocate a government monopoly on education. Yet that is what we are, in fact, approaching."

Change Agents

Many parents are losing faith in the government schools because some schools are embarking on a course for which they were never intended—change agents.

In an article titled "Forecast for the '70s," the *National Education Association Journal* observed in its January 1969 issue: "The roles and responsibilities of teachers will alter throughout the next decade. Future thought suggests that between 1970 and 1980 a number of new assignments and specialties will materialize if present trends continue. For one thing, the basic role of the teacher will change noticeably. Ten years hence it should be more accurate to term him a 'learning clinician.' This title is intended to convey the idea that schools are becoming 'clinics' whose purpose is to provide individualized psychosocial 'treatment for the student.' "

Many of the government-sponsored "alternative schools" are already heavily bent in the direction of "unfreezing old beliefs and attitudes and moving to new socially relevant concepts." Some months ago a *Minneapolis Tribune* news item reported concerning the students from one of these schools: "Probably the most serious development is that some of the students have become worried about whether they are learning basic skills and normal school subjects. . . . They are at a point where they want skilled teachers rather than groovy relators."

You say, but what about the many public schools that are not having all the problems you are talking about, and what about all the teachers who are Christians in public education? First, we ought to thank God for every teacher in public education who is a Christian. It would be a tragedy to envision public schools without them. They have a decided savoring effect even as Christians have on all society. However, there are many obstacles to an effective Christian witness in many public schools.

Secondly, while there are still many safe and sane public schools in the country, every indicator measuring national trends and statements from numerous national leaders points to further deterioration. Seemingly, problems will grow and opportunities for Christian witness will decline. Perhaps it is too early to say that the marriage of more than 100 years between the American people and the public school system is falling apart. But there is strong evidence that they are becoming more and more incompatible.

Speaking to a Christian school audience,
Governor Ronald Reagan said,
"God is not dead on your campuses."

4

Friends
of Christian Schools

In 1966 I had an interview with Dr. Max Rafferty, then the California state superintendent of public instruction. I was new in my job as executive director of the California Association of Christian Schools. For this important meeting, I thought it would help if I took my brother-in-law, Wayne Brown, who is a public school teacher in the Sacramento area—and who, by the way, sends his children to a Christian school. He brought along his recording equipment and also took several pictures. We were both so nervous that we could hardly get the recording machine going.

Dr. Rafferty did his best to calm us and gave us an excellent interview. One of his statements was: "Christian schools teach their children morality and decency, obedience to law and order, respect and courtesy for others, love of country, and obedience to God. That's why private Christian schools are the greatest friends which people who profess my point of view have. I know it. I appreciate it. And I try to help them whenever I can."

And he did! On two occasions, he spoke at CACS state conventions and has, over the years, been a special speaker at Christian school functions around the country. He has also been the speaker at a Parent-Teacher Fellowship meeting of a small Christian school in Folsom, Calif. The parents could hardly believe their eyes when they saw the state superintendent of public instruction on the platform at their Christian school PTF meeting.

Dr. Rafferty was and is a true friend of Christian schools. Other noted men, some of them in public education, are likewise sympathetic or even frankly enthusiastic toward Christian schools.

Paul Harvey, considered by many to be the nation's leading radio newscaster, spoke at a banquet for 800 Christian school educators at the Disneyland Hotel in Anaheim in the spring of 1968. He captivated the audience that night. Not only did he commend Christian school education then, but the following day on his network newscast to millions of listeners, he spoke of the growth of the Christian school movement and the excitement and motivations behind it. It was a thrilling experience for all of us in this work to hear a man of Mr. Harvey's stature share freely his enthusiasm for Christian school education on his American Broadcasting Network news program.

Another friend of Christian schools is California Governor Ronald Reagan. With members of the CACS executive board, I prayed much about asking the governor to speak at the CACS spring rally we had had scheduled at the beautiful new Anaheim Convention Center. We sent our letter of invitation to the governor's office nearly a full year in advance. I received a response from the governor stating that it was too early to determine his schedule for next April. We continued to pray.

One rainy Sunday evening, I was standing in the Pacific Southwest Airlines Terminal at the Los Angeles International Airport waiting my turn to board a PSA flight to Sacramento. I was scheduled to testify on behalf of Christian schools at a legislative hearing the next morning in the capital. As I stood at the window watching the rain, I saw an entourage of police cars and a black limousine come driving up to the plane I was about to board. Before I could fully comprehend it, the governor and his son and bodyguard were walking up the ramp of "my" plane. Because very few of the other waiting passengers saw the governor board the plane, it was easy for me to position myself so I was the first in line to go on board. I seated myself two rows behind him.

I wasn't sure how I was going to go about speaking to the governor, but I had a feeling the Lord arranged this meeting. After we were airborne, and had been flying a few minutes, I handed my calling card to a stewardess and asked her to give it to the governor and tell him I would like to speak with him. This completely flustered her. You would have thought I had given her a note saying I was about to blow up the plane. She immediately handed my card to a male steward. He walked on past the governor with it to the captain's quarters in the cockpit and closed the door behind him. I said to myself, "My calling card has never had this effect on people before!" He came out of the cockpit and handed my card to the governor's bodyguard across the aisle. The guard gave it to the governor. In short order, the guard motioned for me to come up and talk with the governor. And what a gracious gentleman he was! We had a fine conversation. I told him of our plans for the CACS spring rally and asked if he could find time in his busy schedule to speak to us. He said he would check his calendar the next day. He introduced me to his son, we shook hands, and I went back to my seat quietly thanking the Lord for arranging my schedule to meet the governor of California personally at a strategic time when I needed to see him.

Back in my office two days later, I received a call from Pat Gayman, the governor's schedule secretary, saying that Governor Reagan would speak to us!

Upon receiving a beautiful Bible and a plaque from CACS at the rally in April 1969, the governor presented CACS officials with a proclamation declaring the third week of November each year as private education week in California. Then he settled into his speech.

A portion of his address follows:

> Private schools have always had a tremendously important role in our nation and our state's educational system. It's essential to our total education system that private schools thrive. The private institution often serves as a pace setter, an educational whetstone, helping to hone the educational process and forcing the public system to compete in a drive for excellence. And in this day when Dr. Spock's babies have grown up, there is a need for excellence as we have never known before. It's a tribute to the wisdom of the people that they continue to contribute and undergo a kind of double charge for education by sending their sons and daughters to the

institutions you represent and all of this over and above the heavy tax burden which supports public education. The fact that your institutions continue to grow in size and numbers indicates the confidence that the people have that you are filling the need and producing a superior product.

Your institutions are very much needed. You are part of the bulwark of morality that's so essential to the foundations of freedom. History shows that you can't have one without the other. God is not dead on your campuses. As a result of these we will be calling, even leaning on you more heavily in the troublesome times to come. The world is hungry for morality, searching for integrity, and crying for leadership, and none more so than our youth.

The other day on television as we all mourned the death of Dwight Eisenhower, I saw something that chilled me even in that moment of grief. Television was covering a school in our vicinity called the Eisenhower School, and these youngsters had been brought out to the playground to stand there as the flag came down to half mast. And then I heard the principal (and saw it there on television) say to these children, "Now we will all silently bow our heads and meditate for the Eisenhower family." They couldn't even use the word prayer.

Properly directed, the sweeping technological changes in our life ahead can provide great progress. But at the same time there are waves of destructive cultural change heading our way. Today we are told that we've swept aside the dead hand of the past with its constricting and confining tradition and morality. We are told that the discipline of the ages past no longer binds us. We are told that in view of this rapid transformation, all standards are relative to social considerations of man and society. And man and society are whatever mere mortals choose to make of them. Just change itself, just change for the sake of change, becomes the dominant philosophy of the age. To freely discuss on all sides of all questions, without standards, without values, is to insure the creation of a generation of uninformed and talkative minds.

The challenge is to search for progress in a worried world. But the obligation is to help young people find truth and purpose, to find an identity. We can no longer afford to starve the spirit and thus kill the soul.

And let me tell you now, I as one citizen, . . . [look forward to] the day when you will find yourself taking your place in the ranks of education in this land, because your influence is greatly needed there.

May God give us more government leaders who will speak in support of the Christian school ministry. The governor's statements received wide coverage in newspapers and newscasts around the country. In many ways the CACS spring rally was a high point for Christian schools everywhere.

Not the least among the friends of Christian schools are Bible-believing pastors across America who have established Christian schools or who are supporting Christian schools in their area. Among these pastors is Dr. David Hocking, pastor of the First Brethren Church, Long Beach, Calif. The church sponsors its own system of schools called Brethren Church Schools in Long Beach and Paramount—a preschool through high school program for more than 1,000 students. Pastor Hocking is a product of the school his church sponsors. His parents enrolled him in the second grade at the elementary level and he continued on through Brethren High School. He was an honor student throughout his schooling and he went on to college and seminary. He now pastors the 1,700-member church that sponsors the Christian schools he attended. He is a dynamic preacher of the Word. He says:

> My life has been greatly affected by the Christian schools that I now serve as pastor and president. Having gone through our Christian school system and graduated, I found later, in both college and seminary, that the background I received prepared me for the disciplines related to my future ministry in a way that could not have been accomplished without the benefit of that Christian school education.
>
> Our Brethren Church Schools . . . have been used of God in a variety of ways all of which greatly enhance and benefit the ministry of our church.
>
> First, they have created an atmosphere of teaching that parallels for our families what they are taught in our church and thus have helped Christian parents in that responsibility which chiefly belongs to them.
>
> Second, our Christian schools have opened up tremendous opportunities for evangelism both among the students who make application and their parents.
>
> Third, we have reached many [unchurched] families that now are members of our church, and this has continued to add to the overall growth of our church.
>
> Fourth, Christian schools have given us the opportunity to train our young people in a way

that has prepared them for future service for Jesus Christ. Many of these young people who have gone through our schools are now deeply involved in the ministry of our church and some of them are now a part of either our full-time or part-time staff. We do not see our Christian schools as a separate entity of our church, but rather we see them as a church evangelizing and educating through the week.

These friends and a host of others like them are speaking out for Christian schools.

"We believe that God does not cease
to exist from 9 a.m. to 3:30 p.m.
Monday through Friday. . . ."
A California public school teacher

5

Why Many Public School Educators Send Their Own Children to Christian Schools

One of the largest groups among the parents who send their youngsters to Christian schools are public school teachers and principals. In 1973 I conducted a nationwide survey among these public school educators and asked them to write a few words concerning why they send their own children to Christian schools. I think you will find this sampling of their replies interesting!

> After teaching 10 years in public schools, I realized many of my students lacked several things: (1) discipline; (2) reading skills; (3) belief in God; and (4) love of people and country. The Christian school has all of these and more. My child loves her school.
>
> —*A public school teacher who sends her daughter to King's Academy, West Palm Beach, Fla.*

I became a member of the Santa Cruz Board of Education before my children were of school age. Subsequently, two of our children are in Baymonte Christian School. I am tremendously impressed with the impact that is made on a child when the Bible and Christ-oriented exposure become integrated into the learning process.
—*A resident of Santa Cruz, Calif.*

I prefer to send my two children to a Christian school because Christ is central to all information taught and caught. The public school is basically humanistic and materialistic in its approach to life and the fundamental questions of human existence and purpose. The Christian school holds a unique position with the home and the church.
—*A public school social studies teacher whose children attend Emerald Empire Christian School, Eugene, Ore.*

We believe that God does not cease to exist from 9 A.M. to 3:30 P.M. Monday through Friday, but with the laws and trends affecting public education today, this is the atmosphere in which our children would go to school if they attended public schools. We feel that we want as much continuity as we can get in our children's lives. If one thing is emphasized at home but is contradicted (no matter how subtly) at school then we lose a great deal of ground. The religious aspect of our children's lives is the most important reason for having them in a Christian school, but there are sound academic reasons for it too. Public schools have had, in our view, too many experimental and innovative programs which, after the damage has been done, prove to be valueless.

>   —*A seventh- and eighth-grade public school teacher who sends her three youngsters to San Gabriel Christian School, San Gabriel, Calif., and to Maranatha Christian High School, Arcadia, Calif.*

Children are a gift from God, entrusted to parents for proper care and training. As Christian parents, we want Christ to be the center of our children's lives including their education. This can only be done in a Christian school by dedicated Christian teachers who put Christ at the center of their lives and of all subject matter.

>   —*A public school tenth-grade teacher who sends his children to Gloucester Country Christian School in New Jersey.*

Our public schools are required to work with an increasing number of pupils who waste a great deal of time by disruptive behavior. Such pupils are hostile to teachers and classmates and occasionally attack them physically. Their parents may also be hostile to society. They make it difficult or impossible for learning to take place. These unfortunate children need help, but I do not think my children can help them. I want my children to grow and learn in a wholesome, loving atmosphere where parents, teachers, and students work together and Bible study is provided. Sunday School alone, as good as it is, is not enough.

>   —*A public high school teacher who sends her youngsters to Inglewood Christian School, Inglewood, Calif.*

We send our daughter to a Christian school because the environment of the public school she would attend does not promote learning. There is a serious lack of discipline, stealing is very common, and the "pod" idea as it is being administered there is a joke. She is a very bright child, and we feel she should not be deprived of the right to learn.

> —*A fifth-grade public school teacher who sends her daughter to North Florida Christian School, Tallahassee, Fla.*

We send our children to Alma Heights Christian Academy primarily to learn about our Creator and the Holy Bible. There are many advantages to Christian education such as smaller class size, individual attention from warm and understanding people who really care about the whole student, conscientious discipline, and a good feeling of working together to attain God's will in the student's life.

> —*A kindergarten public school teacher who sends her children to Alma Heights Christian Academy, Pacifica, Calif.*

The assumption of the public school is that man is the product of evolution and most teachers accept this as established. Therefore the basic foundations of morality are based on temporal expediency. The Christian school teaches and exemplifies morality based on unchanging truth. The attitude toward the student sharply contrasts. The public school teacher too often looks at the student as a number, the ministry of teaching as a job. Most teachers in the Christian school try to understand the uniqueness of each student.

As a consequence of the above, most graduates of Christian schools are better prepared intellectually and morally to face the problems of adult life.

—A public high school English and social studies teacher who sends his youngsters to Wescove Christian High School, Potomac, Ill.

The social and academic climate of the public junior high school failed to inspire confidence in my husband and me. The "anything goes" culture, with its loose and conflicting standards and indefinite guidelines would have left our children confused and uncertain regarding life's values and expectancies. Our Christian school provides a consistent climate for growth and learning through clearly defined guidelines for values based on the unchanging truths of God's Word. The peace of mind shared with us by our children that their well being in all its forms is the chief concern of our school is worth many times more than the cost of tuition.

—A sixth-grade public school teacher whose children attend Southland Christian Schools, Chula Vista, Calif.

We send our children to a Christian school to supplement the basic principles they are taught at home in real life situations. We also appreciate the fact that wholesome activities are provided for them, and their closest friends are Christians.

—A public school third-grade teacher who sends her children to Mansfield Christian School, Mansfield, Ohio.

"Cease, my son, to hear the instruction
that causeth to err from
the words of knowledge"
(Proverbs 19:27).

6

What's a
Christian Parent
to Do?

As Christian parents search the Scriptures regarding their parental obligation to their children, many conclude that to send their children to non-Christian schools is to violate biblical directives regarding their education. Scriptures such as "Cease, my son, to hear the instruction that causeth to err from the words of knowledge" (Prov. 19:27), and "Train up a child in the way he should go" (Prov. 22:6) are beginning to make an impact on them. Because of the anti-Christian climate and the strange events going on in some public schools, more and more parents are coming to the conclusion that to send their children to public schools is clearly not the way they *should* go. And to place children under the influence of a government-controlled curriculum that does not honor the Lord and does not represent the position of Christian parents is to "hear . . .

instruction that causeth to err from the words of knowledge."

Those may sound like strong statements but consider the following examples of problems in public education. Such problems have affected many Christians as they have contemplated the matter of which school is right for their children.

On October 14, 1973, during a speech in Phoenix, Ariz., Dr. W. P. Shofstall, Arizona state superintendent of schools, said: "The greatest achievement of the devil in America today is the fact that a state superintendent of schools may not legally participate in any activity in a public school building for the purpose of overtly knowing, understanding, and doing the will of God. The atheists have, for all practical purposes, taken over public education in this country."

Shocking words, yes, but they were spoken by a prominent public school educator. Contrast this with the previously cited statement by Governor Ronald Reagan in his address at the 1969 spring rally of the California Association of Christian Schools. In his dramatic manner, he pointed to the audience of nearly 6,000 people, saying, "Your institutions are very much needed. You are part of the bulwark of morality that's so essential to the foundations of freedom. God is not dead on your campuses."

In November 1973, I met a dynamic Christian public school principal who holds a doctorate in education. We met at the Fresno Convention Center, where nearly 2,100 delegates had gathered for the annual teacher's convention of CACS. This public school principal, who sends his sons to one of our Christian schools in the San Francisco Bay area, said he was at the convention because after 23 years of service, he was considering resigning his job in the public school system and starting a Christian school. He made the following statement growing out of his experience in the Bay Area public school system:

The public schools increasingly are becoming militantly secular—beyond that envisioned by the Supreme Court in its decisions concerning the separation of church and state. Humanism is espoused actively, along with militant feminism and disparagement of our government and our traditional values. They promote relative morality, rebellion against authority, and sometimes weird and supernatural practices. The philosophers of the public schools have discovered that it is very difficult to teach children in a vacuum. So they have turned their emphasis away from traditional subject matter toward various schemes for perfecting society and individuals. I know for a fact that children from the kindergarten through high school are propagandized concerning one or more of the above mentioned concepts. Anyone who believes that public schools are academic institutions where children and young people can learn the arts and sciences of civilization in a businesslike way, without the accompaniment of the inculcation of non-Christian ideologies, may be ignorant of what is going on in many geographical areas of our country, particularly at the junior high level of instruction.

My wife and I treasure our boys and we send them to a Christian school so that they will be given the same values and priorities which we have.

His statement about "weird and supernatural practices" in public schools is symptomatic of a problem in a growing number of public schools around the country. While speaking in Syracuse, N.Y. in 1973, I was told by a Christian public school teacher that the North Syracuse school district had introduced a "mini-course in magic." In Worthington, Ohio a high school student who attends a public high school in nearby Columbus told me that her school invited a witch to come to one of her classes. She said the witch arranged the students in a circle on the floor, turned out the lights, placed four candles in the center of the circle and actually involved the students in a séance. Since that time, I have been asking questions in other cities where I have spoken and found similar firsthand accounts in St. Charles, Mo. and several cities in California. As much as we do not want to hear it, witchcraft and the occult are on the rise in public education.

Teachers of Eastern religions are pushing into educational institutions and are knocking at the doors of public schools.

Assemblyman Kenneth Meade of the California Legislature, on April 10, 1973 introduced Assembly Concurrent Resolution Number 66, which declares that the "legislature strongly encourages all educational institutions to include courses in the science of creative intelligence on the campuses and in the facilities; encourages all possible cooperation with the 23 centers for the teaching of the science of creative intelligence; and supports the program of Maharishi International University to establish educational television stations broadcasting educational material to popularize the knowledge and practice of the science of creative intelligence."

Though the resolution failed, it was reportedly to be reintroduced.

In May 1972 the Illinois General Assembly passed a somewhat similar resolution, in this case commending Transcendental Meditation and encouraging universities to supply space for teaching it to help combat drug abuse among students.

At the high school level, Transcendental Meditation is already being taught in "Science of Creative Intelligence" courses in Los Angeles, Santa Barbara, and the Bay Area in California, and reportedly in several other localities across the U.S.

"Transcendental Meditation," according to a release by Citizens for Constructive Education, "is a yoga system taught by the Maharishi Mahesh Yogi. Best known as the ex-guru of the Beatles, the Maharishi is a religious leader who deserves to be taken quite seriously in the light of the world-wide organization he has developed in the last 14 years. Since his first visit to the United States in 1959, over 200,000 persons have been trained in TM in this country. Currently over 10,000 new meditators are initiated monthly at the 200 strategically located centers in the United States. Fees of $35, $45, or $75, respectively, are collected from high school, college, or adult initiates. From these figures it appears that the Maharishi's organization, The Student's International Meditation Society/International Meditation Society (SIMS/IMS), receives half a million dollars a month or six million dollars annually from this source. SIMS is a nonprofit, tax-exempt educational organization."

The continued emphasis on the teaching of the theory of evolution as fact in many public schools creates a moral crisis for Christians. Countless young people who once confessed confidence and faith in God's Word have been negatively influenced by that antibiblical, unscientific theory of the origin of man. Christian schools teach the theory of evolution as a countertheory to the biblical account of creation. It could be said that public school students are "sheltered" from hearing the *biblical* view which, as you think of it, is more believable than the theory of evolution.

Happily, there have been encouraging signs in at least one public school system. The following memo was issued in 1972 by the Texas State Board of Education to all public school teachers in that state:

"You may ridicule the concept of water running uphill; yet you have been forcing students to accept the far more fantastic idea that the universal natural laws of thermal dynamics reverse themselves to accommodate evolution. We remind you that you have the distinct legal and grave responsibility to be truthful and honest, and that you fulfill your responsibility by presenting students with the fact that evolution is an unproved theory and impossible in the minds of many leading scientists of our nation."

But there are other serious problems within public schools, generally. The great nineteenth century scholar Robert Bunsen said, "Culture of intellect, without religion in the heart, is only civilized barbarism and disguised animalism."

Arizona State Superintendent of Schools Dr. Shofstall said in his 1973 Phoenix speech, "Atheism, called humanism, has become the religion of the public schools." He also said: "The greatest heresy of all is the confusion between humanism and theism. Here the devil is most diabolical. If you say to most well-meaning people, 'I am a humanist,' they will usually say, 'Isn't that beautiful!' "

He then quoted from the September-October 1973 issue of *The Humanist* magazine, which reads: "Humanists believe that traditional theism, especially faith in the prayer-hearing God, assumed to love and care for persons, to hear and understand their prayers, and to be able to do something about them, is an unproved and outmoded faith. Salvationism, based on mere affirmation, still appears harmful, diverting people with false hopes of heaven hereafter."

If the above statement represents the philosophy of humanists, and if "atheism, called humanism, has become the religion of the public schools," as Dr. Shofstall claims, then it should not be too surprising that Christian parents by the thousands are seeking Christian schools for their children.

As public education in many areas degenerates in these respects, it is becoming easier for many Christian parents to lay aside the view that it is somehow advantageous to expose children to an anti-Christian educational environment. Consider one major inconsistency in this long standing idea. Working among a variety of Bible-believing churches, I have learned to understand and respect their theological and organizational differences and to rejoice in their common areas of unity. One common feature of many of them is the strong feeling that their particular Sunday School is the best Sunday School in town. All of them believe that they are teaching biblical truth as their children and young people should be taught. Because of their allegiance to truth, most parents in these churches would not likely send their children to a Sunday School of another denominational or theological persuasion. Understandably, they simply are not in the business of recommending other Sunday Schools for fear of leading someone into a less desirable way. We do not question all of this, for as long as churches are filled with mortals, there will always be a great variety of theological thinking.

But isn't it amazing that many of these same conscientious people who draw careful lines regarding churches and Sunday Schools will, on Monday morning, send their own children to a secular educational environment in the public school? Here the teaching is far more spiritually devastating in the span of one week than the combined effect of sending their children to a different Sunday School every Sunday for an entire year. By what devious logic have these Christians persuaded themselves that Johnny is not equipped to withstand the teachings of an alien church but he is somehow capable of withstanding a highly funded, professional, 30-hour-a-week secular educational presentation in the public school? Such a presentation may possibly include one or more of the following: humanism, evolution, witchcraft, transcendental meditation, group morality, and a subtle subversion of parental and biblical authority. Add to that the ever-present pushers of drugs, narcotics, and booze in many schools, and you have, unless you prefer to keep your head in the sand, some good reasons to register some old-fashioned parental concern. If any one of the above topics was given even five minutes of a positive presentation in your child's Sunday School class, the teacher likely would be out the door before the next Sunday! How wondrous, strange and inconsistent we mortals be!

What is a Christian parent to do? More and more Christians are coming to the conclusion that it is time for the Christian community to declare an educational emergency and support an educational program that will not kick the spiritual stuffings out of the next generation.

"The natural rights of a parent to custody and control of . . . children are subordinate to the power of the state to provide for the education of their children. . . . ."

From Ohio Education Code

7

Children—
Whose Responsibility
Are They?

Children—whose responsibility are they? You say with indignation, "Why parents', of course!" Yet there are whole battalions of so-called social scientists and a few liberal educators who will tell you "nose to nose" that children belong to the state. For example, *The Seattle Times* on October 24, 1973 editorialized:

> Imagine a young couple making the decision that it is time to have a baby. But they can't have a child until they go to a government agency and convince the bureaucrats that they deserve a license for parenthood.

> Roger W. McIntire, professor of psychology at the University of Maryland, has a long article in the October 1973 issue of *Psychology Today* in which he urges the licensing of parenthood. His justification . . . is the protection of children.

" 'Our culture makes almost no demands when it comes to the children's psychological well-being and development,' McIntire writes. 'Any fool can now raise a child any way he or she pleases, and it's none of our business. The child becomes the unprotected victim of whoever gives birth to him.' "

Do his words bother you? They should because they are in direct violation of biblical teaching. The psalmist says, "Lo, children are an heritage of the Lord." They are given to parents by the Lord. They are a gift from God; they are not community, state, or federal property. Parents, under God and no one else, are responsible for their children.

The depraved condition of a growing number of irresponsible parents who are harmful to their children is to be deplored. Anyone who has a compassion for children is deeply disturbed by this. What is needed, however, is a spiritual heart transformation in these distraught parents—not the institution of government-controlled parenthood. So many human problems could be solved easily if sinful men and women would, in simple faith, turn to God through Christ and live according to His Word.

Now, let's restate the theme question for this chapter within the context of education. Children—who is responsible for their *education?* You say again, "Why parents are, of course!" Yet here also there is a determined socialistic, anti-Bible segment of our society that believes that children are "an heritage" of the state and that the *state* is responsible for the education of children. This idea has reached such proportions in the U.S. that the State of Ohio has revised its education code to read, in part, as follows:

" . . . The natural rights of a parent to custody and control of . . . children are subordinate to the power of the state to provide for the education of children. Laws providing for the education of children are for the protection of the state itself." (Revised Education Code, page 195, Ohio School Guide, section 7.06, Compulsory Education Law.)

If you believe that the family, under God, is the basic and primary unit of society, then you will agree that the Revised Education Code of Ohio has awesome implications, going beyond compulsory education. We must do everything possible to preserve our rights as parents to maintain the "custody and control" of the children God has given us.

While we still have the legal right to care for our own children, let us be diligent about our privilege as parents.

The State of Ohio notwithstanding, parents are totally responsible for their children. The home environment, churches, schools, and even friends are agencies that function to aid parents in training their children "in the way they should go." Parents, before God and to the best of their ability, are responsible to see to it that these environmental factors conform to the biblical standards of the mental, physical, and spiritual development of their children. And when, in the judgment of parents, the environmental factors of home, church, school, or friends are not conducive to the well-being of their children, parents have a responsibility to improve or change the situation.

Family
If, indeed, the family is the basic unit of society, then society must serve and be subservient to the family's purpose. It is especially important that leaders of

churches and schools understand this principle, because all too often these institutions, as important as they are, have a tendency to use families as though churches or schools were really the basic unit of society.

In this regard, Dr. Howard Hendricks in *Heaven Help the Home!* (Victor Books) questions, "Is it possible that some churches are doing more to break up homes than to build them? Are we engaged in a program of competition with the home, or cooperation?"

In God's Book—the Bible—families are still number one. "If any provide not for his own, and specially for those of his own house, he hath denied the faith, and is worse than an infidel" (1 Tim. 5:8).

Hear Dr. Bill Diem, a dynamic Christian psychologist who for many years has been a counselor to prison inmates who have committed serious crimes. At a special banquet for parents in Diamond Bar, Calif. he said, "The large majority of men in prison with whom I work were at one time youngsters who were not loved and properly disciplined at home, especially by fathers." He laid great stress on fathers being the strong leaders of the household.

As much as a Christian school education is valuable, the home is by far, for better or for worse, the greatest influence in the total environment of youngsters and young people. Dr. Hendricks in *Heaven Help the Home!* says, "The average church has a child 1% of his time; the home has him 83% of his time; and the school for the remainder"—which is 16%. This does not negate nor minimize the need for churches and schools but it dramatizes the fact your home is 83% of your child's world and you've only got one time around to make it good. Get with it!

Church

Unless the families we serve are church-going families, our efforts in Christian school education are seriously handicapped. Someone has said, "Church, home, and school—Christ is all three—the divine ideal." The combination of church, home, and school is a bit like a three-legged stool. If one leg is missing, the stool will fall. The church, therefore, is vitally important to your children's environment. If you insist that your youngsters attend school, you can also insist that they attend Sunday School and church. It is a vital part of your parental responsibility.

School

A brochure of one of our leading Christian schools states: "The Bible teaches that for a Christian, life is not divided into the secular and the sacred. It is not up to the home and church to train the child in 'spiritual' matters while the school teaches him 'secular' subjects. Such a dualistic approach often leads to conflicts and frustrations in the mind of the child when he hears one philosophy at home and church and another at school. 'The teacher says,' or 'the coach says,' carries much weight in the mind of the child. The home and church and the school should all be moving in the same direction with the same philosophy and goals."

The school which your children attend should be an extension of the training program of your home —not of the state or federal government. Please keep in mind that the Christian school is not to take the place of the home. The Christian school is designed to help parents fulfill their Christian responsibility "to train up a child in the way he should go."

Friends

As youngsters progress in school through their upper elementary grades and on into their junior and senior high school years, the influence of close friends often exceeds that of teachers, preachers, and parents combined. Therefore, parents should be concerned about the friends of their children. Since parents are responsible for the total environment of their children, they should help their youngsters select wholesome friends. Parents would do well to fellowship with other parents whose children are the caliber they want their own children to be. The wrong friends for your children can quickly undo the years of parental love and training you have given.

Training your children "in the way they should go" should be the major pursuit of every parent. Beware lest you be caught up in activities less important than the preservation of your children. Paraphrasing Matthew 16:26 we might say, "What shall it profit a parent who gains a world of material and professional acclaim and loses his own family?" Raising your family for Christ must always be number one on your list of life's priorities.

The Christian philosophy of education
calls for an educational process
that puts the Bible at the center
and asks the student and the teacher
to evaluate all they see in the world
through the eyes of God—
because God is Truth.

8

The Christian
Philosophy
of Education

Abraham Lincoln said, "The philosophy of the classroom is the philosophy of the government in the next generation."

Nearly 100 years before Lincoln, George Washington said: "True religion affords government its surest support. The future of this nation depends on the Christian training of the youth. It is impossible to govern without the Bible." For this reason, schools and textbooks of the postcolonial period were Bible oriented.

Dr. Lloyd T. Anderson, pastor of Bethany Baptist Church, West Covina, Calif. says: "We make a mistake when we say that the pilgrims came to America to seek religious freedom. To a certain extent they had this in Holland. It would be more accurate to say that they came to America seeking an opportunity to give to their children the kind of religious education that was impossible in either England or Holland."

For over 100 years, first-graders learned to read from *The New England Primer*. The 1762 edition taught the ABCs this way:

> A—In Adam's Fall, We Sinned All
> B—Heaven to Find, The Bible Mind
> C—Christ Crucify'd, For Sinners Dy'd

The McGuffey Reader series, which replaced *The New England Primer,* had a similar biblical emphasis. Liberal historian Henry Steele Commager acknowledged this in an introduction he wrote for a reissue of *McGuffey's Fifth Reader.* He said:

"What was the nature of the morality that permeated the [*McGuffey*] *Readers?* It was deeply religious, and . . . religion then meant a Protestant Christianity. . . . The world of the *McGuffeys* was a world where no one questioned the truths of the Bible or their relevance to everyday conduct. . . . The *Readers,* therefore, are filled with stories from the Bible, and tributes to its truth and beauty."

Ellwood Cubberly, a prominent educational historian, wrote in his book *Public Education in the United States* (Houghton Mifflin): "The most prominent characteristic of all the early colonial schooling was the predominance of the religious purpose in instruction. One learned to read chiefly to be able to read the catechism and the Bible and to know the will of the heavenly Father. There was scarcely any other purpose in the maintenance of elementary schools."

Commager further points out in his introduction that education and educators have different goals today: "That our children, today, are better taught than were their luckless predecessors is generally conceded, though we are sometimes puzzled that we have not produced a generation of statesmen as distinguished as the founding fathers."

I saw a sign in front of a church recently that said, "It does make a difference what you believe." It does! Our beliefs determine our actions. Even though the curriculum of early American education was limited primarily to reading, writing, arithmetic, and religion, and most of those who attended school went for only two or three years, the impact of the entire curriculum was Bible oriented. The Bible was presented as a point of reference for right and wrong.

Why have we "not produced a generation of statesmen as distinguished as the founding fathers"? Is it because the American educational system over the past 200 years has lost its moral teeth? Now we are "gumming them" with man-made moral platitudes about "honesty is the best policy," implying that man's human behavior sets the standard, with no reference to God's eternal standard. This moral decline is evident in our textbooks.

Dr. John Blanchard, in *Education and the Christian Faith* (Christian School Crusade), reports on a survey that was made several years ago of the reading textbooks used in Massachusetts schools since 1780. The early Massachusetts schools preceded all other public schools. In 1800, it was revealed that spiritual and moral lessons accounted for 99 percent of the content. By 1875, the spiritual and moral content of the readers had been reduced to 50 percent, and as of 1946, less than 1 percent of the material in the readers used in the public schools of Massachusetts had any moral or spiritual content. Dr. Blanchard said, "These figures typify the trend in the content of American textbooks."

More than a century ago when public schools

were first being discussed, noted theologian Dr. A. A. Hodge made this statement: "It is capable of exact demonstration that if every party in the state has the right of excluding from the public schools whatever he does not believe to be true, then he that believes most must give way to him that believes least, and he that believes least must give way to him that believes absolutely nothing, no matter in how small a minority the atheists or the agnostics may be." In light of recent history, that statement takes on the appearance of a remarkably accurate prediction!

The decline in moral content of present-day secular education has prompted Arizona State Superintendent of Schools Dr. Shofstall to say, as mentioned earlier, "Atheism, called humanism, has become the religion of the public schools."

You say, "What in the world happened?" What caused us to slide from a Bible-oriented education to an educational system that has, for the most part, sterilized God out of its curriculum, and in the opinions of at least some Christians who work in public education, has developed into an anti-Christian educational environment? The early American churches, I believe, are at least partially to blame for not offering their Bible-oriented schools to more youngsters in their communities. Only about 10 percent of the colonial children attended school at all. What learning the 90 percent received came from their parents at home and the colonial trade schools. Because the early American churches failed to establish an aggressive teaching and training program, the state and federal governments began a system of education for the masses. The early founders of the public system set the pace philosophically for the new schools. Horace Mann, a

Unitarian Massachusetts lawyer turned educator, is considered the father of public education. Under his leadership, the first teacher training schools were established, and Massachusetts established the first state compulsory school attendance law in 1852.

The first half century of U.S. public education saw the public school pretty much as an extension of the Protestant Church. So much so that the Catholic Church established its own Catholic schools in protest to the "Protestant" public schools.

Protestant influence on public education lost much of its grip during the late '20s and early '30s. During this period, Columbia University became known for its teachers college and for the man who headed the college, philosopher and educator John Dewey, the father of U.S. progressive education. He was a member of the board of the American Humanist Association in 1933—the year it hammered out the first Humanist Manifesto which said that "faith in the prayer-hearing God . . . is an unproved and outmoded faith."

John Dewey, a strong evolutionist and atheist, said, "There is no God and there is no soul. Hence, there are no needs for the props of traditional religion. With dogma and creed excluded, then immutable truth is also dead and buried. There is no room for fixed, natural law or moral absolutes."

Dewey's philosophy of education and the teachers college at Columbia University in New York became the flame from which the torches of other teachers colleges around the country were lit. In short order, Dewey's antifaith, pragmatic, progressive educational philosophy swept through the nation's public school system. Dewey's thoughts and teachings continue to be revered in teacher-training institutions throughout America.

Much of today's Christian school movement is not a return to Puritan methods of education that were characterized by "much memorization and whipping," but it is an effort on the part of Bible-believers to provide an educational program in which Christ is honored and the teachings of God's Word are freely shared with a generation of youngsters who are reaching out for light in a dark world.

Christian schools offer a philosophy of education that is refreshingly different from the secular world of education. Here is one of the clearest and most concise statements regarding the Christian philosophy of education, written by Dr. Roy Zuck, then executive director of Scripture Press Ministries, now on the faculty of Dallas Theological Seminary:

Is there really a "Christian view" of science, literature, and history? Aren't the facts of science, literature, and history the same no matter where they are taught? Yes, the facts are the same. If it's mathematics, it's mathematics. If it's history, it's history.

But it's the interpretation of the facts that makes the difference. Whether my children attend a secular or a public school, they'll learn basically the same facts, but in a Christian school they'll learn to understand, interpret, and analyze those facts from a biblical perspective.

The secular vs. Christian school issue is really a question of whether a child will learn to view life from man's perspective or God's perspective. From man's viewpoint, history is purposeless; from God's viewpoint, history has meaning. From man's viewpoint, science is the laws of "nature" at work; from God's viewpoint, science is the outworking of His laws.

In science, Christian teachers refer to the Creator of the creation. In literature, Christian teachers evaluate man's writings by biblical standards. In music and art, Christian teachers uphold a wholesome expression consistent with Scripture. In health and hygiene, Christian teachers point out that man is God's creation, "fearfully and wonderfully made." In social studies, Christian teachers help students understand God's view of the world's cultures, governments, and problems.

In short, the purpose of the Christian school [as a Florida Christian school principal put it] is "to give the students that added dimension of the realization of God in all of life."

Of course, this means that the biblical viewpoint permeates every subject of knowledge. Adding a few courses in Bible, holding chapel services, or beginning each class with prayer are helpful, but do not by themselves make a Christian school. A Christian school requires a scriptural point of view for the entire curriculum.

Dr. Roy Lowrie, one of the great Christian school educators in America and a popular convention and conference speaker, illustrates the Christian philosophy of education before his audiences by holding up the Bible. Then, just beyond the Bible, he holds a textbook. He then tells his audience that the Christian philosophy of education requires that we see everything in life through God's Word—even our textbooks. He says, "If our textbooks do not agree with the teachings of God's Word, then our textbooks are wrong and God's Word is right." He further says, "For Christian school educators, God's Book—the Bible—is not on trial. But every other book, every idea of man, and every philosophy of this world is on trial. They are not on trial by our standards, but by God's standards."

This illustration reminds us of the Apostle Paul's admonition to bring "into captivity every thought to the obedience of Christ" (2 Cor. 10:5).

The late Dr. Mark Fakkema, in the foreword of his *Christian Philosophy* lecture series, said: "Truth is not necessarily truth because it is regarded as such by contemporary scholarship. By way of verifying His statements, our Lord did not appeal to the recognized leadership of His day. Our Lord constantly quoted Scripture as His authority. God's Word is the test of all truth. All teaching that is expressive of God's Word is the test of all truth. All teaching that is expressive of God's Word is true. Teaching that is not expository of the Word is falsehood."

Therefore, the Christian philosophy of education calls for an educational process that puts the Bible at the center and asks the student and the teacher to evaluate all they see in the world through the eyes of God—because God is Truth. All must conform to Him or it is not truth. Jesus said, "I am the Way, the Truth, and the Life" (John 14:6). In true Christian education, students learn to use the Bible to evaluate all of life. The Bible is Life—it is the living Word—it is above every other book.

Needless to say, Christian education is the exact opposite of secular education. *Webster's New Collegiate Dictionary* defines secularism as 'rejection or exclusion of religion and religious considerations" or simply stated, "without God." It is important to note that the definition of atheism is "no God." Secular education ignores or denies God and there is every indication the system is producing a generation that ignores and denies God.

The Christian philosophy of education is more

than an education that is based upon religion; it is itself religious. True Christian education teaches that the natural world takes on meaning only through the supernatural resources of God. Christian school educators are attempting to give Christ His rightful place in education. Jesus Himself was a teacher. We attempt to teach as He taught and is still teaching us today through His Word. There is no higher form of education than Christ-centered Christian education.

Every level of Christian education
is equally important.

9

At What Age Is
Christian Education
Most Important?

Dr. Lloyd R. Simmons, former president of California Baptist College, said, "By what devious mode of logic . . . have we persuaded ourselves that there is scriptural authority for Christian education on the college level, but no corresponding obligation for formal Christian schooling below college age? Every scriptural text used to reinforce Christian education on one level will apply with equal force on every other level."

Over the years, I have worked shoulder to shoulder with Christian educators at all levels: preschool, elementary, junior high, senior high, and college. Nearly all of these educators feel their particular level of education is the most important field of service. That is understandable, because all of these people are deeply committed to their work. I believe there are important reasons for youngsters

77

to have the advantage of Christian education at every level. I agree wtih Dr. Simmons that if Christian education is valid at one level, it is valid at every other level.

It has been my privilege on two occasions to be invited to the inauguration of a college president and march in the academic procession. These are always impressive events, comparable in pageantry to a royal wedding. Neighboring college presidents, college deans, and academic representatives don their impressive black gowns and their square mortarboards, and march across the campus in academic cadence into the college auditorium to hear the new president deliver his inaugural address. Congratulatory messages from impressive individuals pour in from near and far. Events of this magnitude draw television and newspaper coverage as well as mention in numerous publications across the country. I think all of this is important. It officially establishes the incoming president as the new academic and spiritual leader of the college. This is especially important these days when we have a watered-down image of authority figures in general.

The point, however, is that while we have given considerable social status to the installation of, and the position of, a college president, as indeed we should, we give almost no recognition to the installation of leaders of the educational institutions that make it possible for Johnny ever to arrive at college. Not once in all my years in Christian education have I been invited to the installation of a Christian school principal. Unfortunately, the installations of principals, headmasters, superintendents, or early childhood leaders are of such small consequence that they seldom attract more than second-page notice in the town's weekly gazette. I would like to change all of that; I would like to see a similar celebration accompany the installation of Christian school leaders that attends the inauguration of a new Christian college president, because I believe every level of Christian education is equally important.

Christian Preschool

Early childhood education has perhaps the least status inside and outside the Christian community, but it is a level of education that is growing faster than any other. You say, "Preschool youngsters should be home with their mothers!" True, but a high percentage of mothers who have preschool children now work; this is a fact of life we cannot change. Add to that the ever growing number of divorced mothers who must work, and you come face to face with the reality that preschools are a necessary part of our present-day world. When I hear of the plans and objectives of some mind-changing guru social planners and of what they plan to do with preschool children, I say let's get going with Christian preschools!

Eunice Dirks, the CACS director of early childhood education, the first person in the nation to work in a full-time advisory capacity to more than 100 Christian preschools, has provided the following vital information:

Dr. Benjamin S. Bloom of the University of Chicago, head of the Research Conference on Education sponsored by the United States Office of Education, has surveyed over 1,000 individuals who were repeatedly observed and measured from early childhood to adulthood. He says: "Half the intellectual capacity of an adult has been developed by the age of four, and 80 percent by age eight. After that, regardless of schooling and environment, mental abilities can be altered only by 20 percent. After 17, grade 12, intellectual or organized thinking patterns grow at a slow pace."

The late Dr. Bernice T. Cory, cofounder, with her husband, of Scripture Press, writing in *Christian Education Monographs,* pointed out:

"Educators and scientists are affirming that a child's learning and remembering abilities are greater during his preschool years than they will ever be again. According to these specialists, the first five or six years of a child's life are his most sensitive, receptive, and crucial period of development—in fact, the optimum learning period of his entire life! These years are the most critical in which to develop his will to learn, his creativity, and his ability to perform. They affect all his subsequent learning."

She listed the following headlines:

> FIRST FIVE YEARS SHAPE ALL OF LIFE
> EARLY LEARNING FOUND VITAL
> BEHAVIOR IS SET BY AGE FIVE
> TRAIN CITIZENS IN THE CRADLE
> DON'T WAIT FOR THE SCHOOL BELL
> AGE FIVE IS OLD PSYCHOLOGICALLY
> CHILDREN UNDER SIX ARE APT LEARNERS

Arnold Gesell, in his article, "The First Five Years of Life" wrote, "From birth to five or six years, one's life moves at a furious pace, never to be equaled in a like period."

Dr. George W. Beadle, president of the University of Chicago, said, "We may be missing the boat in our educational systems, for we have been ignoring the child's most sensitive and receptive period of development." He also said, "Early learning is much more significant than we had previously thought."

These statements should impress us with the fact that, if the crusade for a youngster's intellectual development is half over by age five, then Christian preschools have the potential of laying some very important spiritual and intellectual foundations upon which to build in later years.

Christian Elementary School

Christian school education in the elementary years is also important because elementary students are most receptive spiritually and are developing the all-important reading, writing, and math skills that make up the basic tool box for learning. Without these tools, a youngster's academic career is seriously handicapped.

Sometimes parents "use" Christian schools. This is perhaps done more in the elementary grades than in any other level of education. Because Christian schools are known for their emphasis on basic skills, some parents, without the knowledge of the school principal at the time of enrollment, send their children to Christian elementary schools up through second or third grade, then transfer them to public schools. This always is a disappointment because these parents have missed the primary purpose of a Christian school education.

Unless a child is inculcated with the Christian school educational philosophy (seeing all one encounters in life through the eyes of God as revealed in God's Word) during his early years, it is a difficult rethinking process later. As we have already seen, patterns of learning are established very early in life.

Christian Junior High School

Mrs. Beatrice Rood, principal of Valley Christian

Junior High School, San Jose, Calif., is a most dynamic junior high school principal. For her, there is no more important level of Christian school education than that of junior high youngsters. She and David Wallace, superintendent of the Baymonte Christian Schools, Santa Cruz, Calif., and I were flying on a 727 jet from San Jose to the Hollywood/Burbank airport for the monthly board meeting of CACS. David Wallace is one of the nation's leading Christian school educators. More than 1,400 students attend the Christian schools he has founded in the San Jose-Santa Cruz area near San Francisco. As we flew, we discussed the topic: At what age is Christian education most important?

As the discussion got underway, I said, "I would like to tape this for release on "Christian School Comment," my daily radio program heard on a number of stations throughout California. I taped as we flew.

David Wallace held that the elementary education levels were the critical years and presented a number of arguments I have already stated. Beatrice Rood pointed out that junior high students are at a critical age, somewhat between worlds. They know they are not adults, and they are doing their best not to appear as children. It is an unsettled, uneven time for them emotionally and physically. The average Sunday School, it is estimated, loses 45 percent of its pupils when they reach junior high age. Peer pressure is at an all-time high during these brief years. Mrs. Rood felt that if there is ever a time for the stabilizing influence of a Christian school it is at the junior high level.

Christian High School
Now what about the importance of Christian high

schools? Three years ago, CACS conducted a survey among 25 Christian high schools and found that 88 percent of their graduates entered college. This was 20 percentage points higher than California public high schools. My survey further revealed that 55 percent of those going on to college chose Christian colleges.

One Christian college president, Dr. Richard Chase, president of Biola College, told me that a full third of his student body now comes from Christian high schools and that they are generally among his better students. He said, however, they present a problem. They know so much more Bible than incoming students from secular high schools that his college is considering offering Bible qualifying exams. If Christian high school graduates can pass them, and he thinks many can, they will be advanced to upper level courses.

I am sure that if we had the privilege of sitting across the table from the scores of Christian high school principals from around the country, they would emphasize a whole host of valid considerations regarding the importance of Christian high school education. Here are four of them:

1. As Christian parents, you want your high school youngster "to evaluate life from a biblical perspective, to interpret the world from a scriptural vantage point, to be prepared for witness in our secular society by being equipped with spiritual armor" (Dr. Roy Zuck). A public high school does not do that. It can't!

2. High school youngsters need the friendship and fellowship of other Christian high school students. These are the dating years. The options, while not always perfect, are significantly better.

3. Christian high students enjoy a "family

feeling" at school. Smaller classes bring about a closer relationship between students and teachers. Smaller student bodies increase the option of participation in student council, government, sports programs, and music and drama activities. There is a sense of belonging in a Christian high school that intensifies a student's feeling of value to himself and to others.

4. The Christian teachers and administrators in a Christian high school are on your side. They are, generally, dedicated, competent, godly, upright, and gracious people who are personally concerned about the spiritual and academic progress of each student. By contrast, some non-Christian teachers in secular schools are exerting an undesirable influence on high school students daily by their own questionable moral standards and their anti-Christian perspective on life.

Christian College

My duties in the Christian school ministry include recruiting Christian teachers for Christian schools. It has been my privilege, as a result, to speak throughout America in college chapel services and to lecture to many education classes. When I compare these Christian colleges with the campus atmosphere at state colleges and universities, I thank the Lord for Christian colleges.

Nearly everything mentioned in this chapter regarding the value of Christian education applies at the college level as well. Combine these features with the fact that college young people are at an age when they often choose a marriage partner and their life's work, and you have good reasons why a Christian college education is vitally important.

Manoah asked the Lord regarding his son, Samson, "How shall we order the child, and how shall we do unto him?" (Jud. 13:12) Why not answer that question about your children with the determination to provide Christian education for them at every level?

Johnny not only needs discipline;
he wants discipline at home and
at school.

10

Do Christian
Schools Care
About Discipline?

Do Christian schools care about discipline? Yes, but not to the extreme of cruel punishment, nor the other extreme of "everybody doing his own thing." A major reason the Christian school movement is the fastest growing educational movement in America is that Christian schools are attempting to bring back some middle-of-the-road "normalcy" to the process of your child's education.

In the previously cited 1973 article on the Christian schools explosion, *U.S. News and World Report* says: "There is rising alarm of parents over what they see as academic laxity in the public schools, along with rampant misbehavior—robbery, drug abuse, and classroom disruption. What these parents are seeking, it is said, is a learning environment for their youngsters that is more disciplined and more religious than can be found in any public school."

During the infamous year of 1852 a colossal attempt was made to bring about the beginning of the end of Bible-oriented education that had been so characteristic of the American classroom—especially up through the *McGuffey Reader* years. In 1852, as previously mentioned, Horace Mann convinced the Massachusetts Legislature to provide "free" education for everybody. He told them that "education for all" would save the taxpayers money because the messianic nature of education would redeem society to the point they could literally empty all the jails and prisons.

Regrettably, Horace Mann is not here today to witness the outcome of his erroneous thinking. Not only is government-sponsored public school education the largest single expense for taxpayers, but our jails and prisons are bursting at the seams. Education by itself is not a redemptive force. Generation after generation of Americans have since been subjected to anti-Christian behavioristic philosophies that daily undermine everything for which Bible-believing families stand.

The behavioristic philosophy is as follows: (1) Man is supreme (therefore there is no higher power); (2) man evolved from lower forms of life (therefore there was no act of creation); (3) man is an animal (therefore he does not have a soul); (4) man is inherently good (therefore is not in need of the Saviour); (5) common practice sets the standard (therefore there are no moral absolutes); (6) criminals are merely antisocial (therefore they are not sinners); (7) "maladjustment" explains all adverse human behavior (therefore there is no such thing as guilt); and (8) bad environment is to blame for all evil (therefore man is not responsible).

You ask, "What does all of this have to do with

discipline?" Your philosophy of the nature of man greatly determines your philosophy of the discipline of man. If you believe that your Johnny came into this world with a human nature that is morally good, your view is in direct contradiction to the teachings of God's Word, which says, "The heart is deceitful above all things and desperately wicked" (Jer. 17:9). You will also have serious reservations about administering discipline to Johnny, who you believe is on his merry way to perfection. Don't you believe it! Johnny not only needs discipline; he wants discipline at home and at school.

Dr. James C. Dobson, author of the best seller *Dare to Discipline* (Tyndale House), is a strong supporter of Christian school education. His daughter attends San Gabriel Christian School in California. In his book, Dr. Dobson cites an interesting incident regarding a child's need for knowing the boundaries:

"During the early days of the progressive education movement, one enthusiastic theorist decided to take down the chain-link fence that surrounded the nursery school yard. He thought the children would feel more freedom of movement without that visible barrier surrounding them. When the fence was removed, however, the boys and girls huddled near the center of the play yard. Not only did they not wander away, they didn't even venture to the edge of the grounds."

Dr. Dobson continues, "There is security in defined limits." Children want discipline, and don't let some leader from the progressive education establishment tell you otherwise.

Children at home and at school respond to discipline if it is administered in love. Early in my ministry as executive director of CACS, I conducted a series of workshops for Christian school teachers in 14 areas of California. The topic of the workshop series was "Discipline in the Christian School." As I traveled from city to city and discussed this topic with several hundred Christian school teachers, three interesting facts about Christian school discipline began to emerge:

(1) Students are less of a discipline problem in school if they have received Christ as Saviour because they are at ease within themselves and are better adjusted individuals. The miraculous transformation of salvation makes a dramatic difference in the total outlook of a youngster.

(2) Students are less of a discipline problem in school if their parents consistently demonstrate love for them in words, actions, and example. The best behaved youngsters ordinarily come from homes filled with genuine parental love—the kind of love that says, "I love you too much to allow you to do something that I know will hurt you." This kind of love sets reasonable limits and sticks to them.

(3) Students are less of a problem in school if parents and teachers will reinforce one another regarding Johnny's behavior at school. If the image and authority of either is diminished by the other, Johnny will naturally take the road of least resistance and the whole system breaks down.

Christian schools care about discipline because without it students learn little except to hate school. Teachers who maintain order are the teachers who are most respected and long remembered. In *Dare to Discipline,* Dr. Dobson says: "A teacher who controls a class without being oppressive is almost always loved by her students. . . . Children admire strict teachers because chaos is nerve-racking. Screaming and hitting and wiggling are fun for about 10 minutes; then the confusion begins to get tiresome and irritating."

Christian schools care about discipline because God cares about discipline. The writer to the Hebrews says, "For those whom the Lord loves He disciplines, and He scourges every son whom He receives. It is for discipline that you endure; God deals with you as with sons; for what son is there whom his father does not discipline?" (Heb. 12:6-7, NASB).

There is no other group of schools
in America
that can speak so freely
about our country's Bible-believing
beginnings as
our country's Bible-believing schools.

11

Do Christian
Schools Care
About Patriotism?

A Christian public school teacher came into my office
and asked for an application to teach in one of our
350 California Christian schools. She handed me a
letter from her assistant superintendent of public
schools, one line of which reads, "You are requested
to refrain from any future use of the Bible."

Perhaps you are thinking she used the Bible
openly to "evangelize" the students. This was not
the case. The teacher told me: "National Educators
Fellowship has produced a plexiglass plaque for sale
to teachers which is called 'Great Thoughts.' On occasions I have quoted George Washington, Andrew
Jackson, Abraham Lincoln, Dwight Eisenhower, or
Thomas Jefferson from these 'Great Thoughts' and
shown the plaque to the students. These are not my
sayings, but direct historic quotes from great Americans. On three occasions, principals have asked me

to remove the plaque from my desk and in each case I obeyed immediately and politely."

Among the sayings of Abraham Lincoln on the plaque is his reference to the Bible. He said, "Take all of this Book upon reason that you can, and the balance on faith, and you will live and die a happier man."

Perhaps even more disheartening for this Christian public school teacher was the fact that she was reprimanded for her lesson on the Washington Monument. Evidently there was no complaint about her description of its height, width, origin, and construction. She said, "The cause for excitement was my reading some of the quotations on the 190 carved tribute blocks set in the inner walls of the descending stairway." Some of the quotations are:

"The heavens declare the glory of God; and the firmament showeth His handiwork."

—Psalm 19:1

"Nature is the art of God."

—Sir Thomas Browne

"Thank God, I—I also—am an American."

—Daniel Webster

"Wisdom is the principal thing; therefore get wisdom: and with all thy getting, get understanding."

—Proverbs 4:7

"Or the concern might have been from finding out that the top of the marble obelisk is an aluminum capped marble pyramid with the inscription, 'Praise be to God,'" the teacher continued. "The principal suggested that if I shared any more of the national monument material, maybe I had better not say any of the quotes were from the Bible."

I don't know how all of this affects you but it makes me appreciate more than ever the freedoms we have in Christian school education that are obviously no longer available in many government-sponsored public schools.

During the years I have served as executive director of CACS, I have visited hundreds of Christian school classrooms. Many times I have joined in the student salutes to the American flag, the Christian flag, and to the Bible.

The Bible is not the most dreaded book in our classrooms as is the case in many public schools. Scores of Christian school choirs sing of their love and loyalty to God and country. Student speakers in our schools extol the virtues of the American ideal and reiterate without fear of school censorship the noble Christian heritage of our beloved land.

Christian school teachers teach their history lessons and enjoy the freedom of sharing the complete "unsecularized" story of the landing of the Pilgrims at Plymouth Rock. They can tell the whole truth about the origin of our country without sterilizing the biblical and Christian references out of it. For example, they can quote an early American pilgrim who wrote, "We came with one and the same end and aime, namely, to advance the kingdom of our Lord Jesus Christ, and to injoy the liberties of the Gospell in puritie with peace." They quote the gentle Puritan poet, George Herbert, who said, "Religion stands on tiptoe in our land, ready to pass on the American strand."

Christian school teachers can and are encouraged to quote such outstanding Americans as Noah Webster who said:

> "The principles of republican government have their origin in the Scriptures.
>
> The Christian religion is the most important and one of the first things in which all children

under a free government ought to be instructed.

The Christian religion must be the basis of any government intended to secure the rights and privileges of a free people.

All government originates in families, and if neglected there, it will hardly exist in society. . . . The foundation of all free government and of all social order must be laid in families, and in the discipline of youth. . . . The education of youth [is] an occupation of more consequence than making laws and preaching the Gospel, because it lays the foundation on which both law and Gospel rest for success."

Do Christian schools care about patriotism? Yes, because the freedoms in education that were dear to our early forefathers are the freedoms that are still available to Christian school educators today. There is no other group of schools in America that can speak so freely about our country's Bible-believing beginnings as our country's Bible-believing schools. The government-sponsored public schools with their philosophies of "separation of church and state" have locked themselves out of the privilege of telling their students the truth about the rich Christian heritage of our country.

Do Christian schools care about patriotism? Yes, because this nation more than any other affords us the opportunity to provide our youngsters a Christian school education—an education that includes a patriot's dream of a land where people love their flag, love their country, and are not afraid to say and to sing "God Bless America."

The Christian school educational
environment is not perfect . . .
but . . . it is nearer
what God would have us provide
for our children
than is available in the secular
educational world,
where God and His Word
are not welcome.

12

Who Is
Sheltered?

Sheltered. This word often comes up in relation to Christian school education. What is the answer to the question, "Are students in a Christian school sheltered?"

If one's definition of a "sheltered child" is a child who is out of touch with the world, a child who never meets a non-Christian at school, a child who will falter at every future temptation, or a child who is subjected to an inferior academic curriculum, the answer is no.

However, the answer is "yes" if one's definition of sheltered includes providing an educational environment that teaches Christian morality, love of country, respect for law and order, and an appreciation for the property and well-being of others. The Christian school environment is a positive environment, one that inspires characteristics and attitudes that are traditional to America's greatness.

Dr. Roy Zuck was not always a believer in the idea of Christian school education. He writes:

> I reasoned that Christians should seek to influence the public school system and not withdraw to cloistered schools. After all, I thought, how could a child learn to live for God in a secular world if he is confined only to a Christian environment? When would he learn to adjust to today's world? Wouldn't it be harmful for him to be sheltered in a "hot-house" environment?
>
> Then I realized a serious mistake in my logic. A hothouse is beneficial, not harmful, to young tender plants! They need protection, care, and nurture in their early days. This helps them become strong and sturdy. Likewise, children need the protection, care, and nurture of a Christian environment.

Dr. Mark Fakkema wrote: "We do not put young plants in hothouses to make them weak. We put them there because they are weak—too weak for outdoor exposure. . . . To train our children in the Christian home and then expose them to non-Christian training in a secular school is as nonsensical as to keep a house plant in the proper temperature in the house for part of the time and then to expose it to freezing temperatures outside the house for the rest of the time!"

In the foreword to this book, Paul Harvey refers to the idea that students in the *public* schools are sheltered. He says they are "sheltered from religious instruction and exposed to all forms of non-Christian philosophy and behavior."

Dr. Roy Lowrie, in an article in *Christian School Comment* entitled "Students Sheltered from the Real World in the Public School System," wrote:

Over a period of years, many parents have talked to me about enrolling their children in the Delaware County Christian School, where I have served as headmaster. They are concerned about the education of their children and raise perceptive questions. The question asked more than any other is this, "Will I be sheltering my children if I send them to the Christian school?" Perhaps that question can be answered in a new manner by looking at some ways in which students are sheltered in the public school system, none of which is true in the Christian school.

Students in the public school are sheltered from the real world. An introduction to the real world begins with an introduction to God. God is, and He can be known. But public school children are not taught this, and they miss the real world in their education.

Another part of the real world is understood when a student learns that God made the universe. The Bible is explicit about this. The teaching of evolution shelters public school students from the real answers about the origin of the universe. Science teachers who are not creationists are sheltering students from reality.

Sheltering occurs when public school students are not taught that man is made by God. God made Adam out of the dust of the ground; then He made Eve out of Adam. And, every baby from Cain until today is just as much the creation of God as Adam and Eve. It is sheltering to teach that man is an animal.

Public school students are sheltered when they are taught that man is basically good. The real world shows that man is basically evil; something is inherently wrong and is not changed by education or environment. The front page of to-day's newspaper will depict the human heart and reveal its depravity. Students do not see this real problem when there is no teaching about sin.

When the Gospel is not taught, students are sheltered from real life in the real world as God wants them to experience it. The Gospel is not taught in the public school classroom. As a result, students are sheltered from the reality of salvation through Jesus, and do not know that God will give them a new heart, with forgiveness of their sins.

Saving faith in Jesus comes from learning the Bible. Public school students are sheltered from this book, apart from excerpts studied as litera-ture. The words of life are kept from them. The Bible gives the answers to the questions and to the problems of the real world but instead of God's Word, students are taught false answers derived from numerous philosophies. Because of these philosophies, they try various lifestyles to face the real world. Sadly, those lifestyles some-times spoil their lives beyond repair.

Public schools shelter students from two im-portant elements for good citizenship. First, prayer for government leaders. God rules today in the kingdoms of men and He tells us to pray for government leaders. Second, respect for civil authority because government is ordained by God. These are high concepts of citizenship and patriotism.

In public schools where the Bible is not taught, students are sheltered from the moral standards required in the real world. They are not taught any moral absolutes, but are taught to make decisions according to that particular situation. God's standards are the best for life in the real world. To live by His moral absolutes is to be free, not bound. It simply is not true that living by God's standards is to miss out on life.

Public school students are sheltered from the reality of divine guidance. God is not considered in establishing relationships with the family, within the class, within the school, within the community. Neither is God's leading sought in the important choices of marriage and career. Guidance is on the humanistic level only.

The best education to prepare a child for the real world is an education in which Jesus Christ is central. The Christian understands the real world and wants to prepare his child for it. Enrolling your children in the Christian school does not mean that you are a crusader against the public school system. It means that you want an education for your child that cannot be given by the public school. Parents send their children to the Christian school because they do not want them sheltered from the real world.

The Apostle Paul, speaking to the Romans, said, "Be not conformed to this world but be ye transformed by the renewing of your mind" (Rom. 12:2). In a very real sense, Christian youngsters who attend non-Christian schools are not being *adjusted* to the world, they are being *conformed* to it. Paul further states, "Be wise in what is good, and innocent in what is evil" (Rom. 16:19, NASB). Again Paul says, "Whatsoever things are pure, whatsoever things are lovely, whatsoever things are of good report; if there be any virtue, and if there be any praise, think on these things" (Phil. 4:8, NASB). Somehow these verses do not support the idea that we are to expose our youngsters and young people to an antifaith environment. There is not one scriptural admonition that tells us to involve our children in an educational environment that does not bring honor to the Lord's name.

The Christian school educational environment is not perfect; it is not heaven-on-earth. There are moments when it is less than desirable. But even with its shortcomings, it is nearer what God would have us provide for our children than is available in the secular educational world where God and His Word are not welcome.

Because Christian schools, for the
most part, must purchase their textbooks
from secular publishers . . . ,
Christian schools must choose
their textbooks carefully.

13

Christian Schools
Choose Their
Textbooks Carefully

Theodore Roosevelt said, "To train a man in mind and not in morals is to train a menace in society."

Early American textbooks were dominated by biblical morality. The most notable of the early texts as mentioned previously, were *The New England Primer* and *McGuffey's Eclectic Reader*. William Holmes McGuffey said, "The Ten Commandments and the teachings of Jesus are not only basic but plenary." These textbooks, widely used until 1900 (120,000,000 copies sold), directly and indirectly taught school children that all truth is of God.

In his booklet *Education and the Christian Faith,* Dr. John Blanchard wrote: "During this period in American education . . . the order of mathematics and the sciences was a reflection of God's divine order; the very existence of man was the result of the direct creative act of God; the record of history was interpreted in the light of divine providence in the affairs of men; the highest use of skills and knowledge was in the service of God and one's fellow man; and finally, all of life was a stewardship for which we must finally give account in accordance with certain eternal principles given to us by God. In brief, God had been the unifying, integrating, and permeating fact during the early years of American education."

As public schools came on the scene a little more than 100 years ago, Horace Mann, secretary of the Massachusetts State Board of Education, began a movement to secularize American education. The transition from sacred to secular did not occur overnight. For nearly a century, the Bible was read daily and prayers were offered in many classrooms. The textbooks, however, were gradually sterilized of biblical content and religious teachings. Public school textbooks, for many years, carried an image of neutrality regarding things spiritual. The image of neutrality is now beginning to fade rapidly, especially in the areas of science, social studies, and literature.

Because Christian schools, for the most part, must purchase their textbooks from secular publishers, whose primary market is the secular schools, Christian schools must choose their textbooks carefully. For example, in the area of social studies, Christian schools avoid such textbooks as the *Promise of America* series, published by Scott Foresman and Company, a major source for books for public schools.

I ran across this series of books in 1972 while speaking in St. Charles, Mo. After a meeting in one of the local churches, which was starting its own Christian school, a woman asked if I had heard of the new *Promise of America* series of social studies textbooks for junior high school students. The title sounded warmly partriotic to me, but I had never heard of it.

"Then I must show you," she said. She later got the five books in the series and showed them to the pastor, his wife, and me.

"These were not easy to obtain," she began. "When my son told me about these new social studies books, I went to his teacher and asked to see them. The teacher replied, 'I'm sorry, but you'll have to talk with the principal about that.' I could not believe what the principal told me. He said, 'I'm awfully sorry, Ma'am, but we do not show these books to parents.'"

A bit sheepishly, with the pastor sitting there, she said, "I don't know if I should have done it, but while the teacher was not in my boy's room, I went in and 'borrowed' one copy of each of the series and here they are."

It soon became evident to the three of us why these books were withheld from the eyes of the parents. We were shocked at the open profanity and various forms of gutter language. The mother had marked several passages. The books advocated the legalization of abortion and marijuana. These were presented as projected "social accomplishments" in the year 2,000. The books promote public nudity, civil disobedience, socialism, draft dodging, and rebellion against parents. In the very first book the church was linked with some strangely worded early Puritan sermons and later on with the Klu Klux Klan. Needless to say, parents, the church, and God do not fare very well in the series. The mother who was showing the books told us she had learned that the *Promise of America* series had been introduced to 30,000 junior high school students in public schools the previous year!

Sometimes it is impossible, but Christian school educators try to avoid textbooks that tell our students that morality is decreed by *groups* or that their personality is formed by *groups* or that they are to conform to the standard of *groups*. Group morality is subtly woven into many textbooks these days.

Christian schools set goals to teach students that each Christian must say to himself: "I am an individual, God-created, and important. I am individually responsible for my own actions. My salvation is individual. I am more than a mere member of a huge body called the 'state.' I am an individual serving truth, and my God is Truth. I am reconciled to my God through faith in Jesus Christ. Don't try to control me through collective guilt. My sins are individual, and through Christ my sins are forgiven. I am not accountable to the collective wisdom of a group, I am individually accountable to the Lord Jesus Christ and the teachings of His Word."

Christian schools use many of the same textbooks that are used in the public schools. Not all of them are bad. As a matter of fact, many of them are excellent and, of course, beautifully produced. At this point in time, very few student texts, especially at the junior high level are like the *Promise of America* series. There are more of them at the high school level and scores of them at the college level. Naturally, Christian schools avoid books that openly attack the church, subtly undermine parents, and attempt to destroy the spiritual, political, and economic foundations of our country.

A growing number of scholarly Christian school

educators are writing textbooks and curriculum materials, and Christian publishers are responding to the challenge. We need more. As secular textbooks deteriorate and reflect the depravity of society, we need textbooks that will show the causes of man's depravity and the hope for a society that will trust in God.

No Christian school administrator
sits in his office and gleefully whistles
a happy tune as he writes out
the school dress code.

14

What about
Dress Codes?

Dress codes—every school has them and nobody likes them. Even public schools have their outer limits that stop the "wacky wonders" who would come to school clad only in their imaginations if somebody didn't blow the whistle on them. We have a few in our town who go to the local public high schools in their bathing suits, which I suppose is what it takes these days to appear out of the ordinary.

I know of no Christian school administrator who sits in his office and gleefully whistles a happy tune as he writes out the school dress code. And it is even less enjoyable to enforce one. I have never known a principal in recent years to run for a major political office—his role of enforcing the school dress code would make it impossible for him to find any backing. That is a bit facetious, I know, but it's an uphill battle for any school administrator to en-force dress codes. You say, "Why brother? Why draw any lines at all? Let the kids wear what they will."

Someone has said, "The sum of the wisdom of the ages is to find out which way God is going and follow Him." At the very heart of Christian educa-tion is the idea of seeing the world around us through the eyes of God as revealed in His Word. If we are to evaluate all of life by a biblical perspective then we should prepare ourselves and our students to in-terpret the world, including the current fads and fashions in light of what Scripture has to say about them.

There is, of course, nothing wrong with a style change. Fashions will change from generation to generation. And because we all want to be ac-cepted by others (especially true among youngsters), we have a strong tendency to follow fashion. This is quite acceptable as long as the fashion we are following does not violate biblical principles.

The Bible does not say precisely what kind of clothes a Christian student should wear, giving room to follow fashion whenever it is morally acceptable. But the Bible states that Christian young people should be "an example of believers" (1 Tim. 4:12) and that the Christian girl must dress modestly (1 Tim. 2:9). Most leaders also agree that there are scriptural guidelines that call for boys to appear masculine and for girls to dress and wear their hair in a feminine manner.

Many leaders of the Christian school community believe that Deuteronomy 22:5 should be applied to the manner of dress of boys and girls: "The woman shall not wear that which pertaineth unto a man, neither shall a man put on a woman's gar-ment; for all that do so are abomination unto the

Lord thy God." When it comes to the controversial topic of hair, these leaders find guidance in Paul's writings. "If a man have long hair, it is a shame unto him, but if a woman have long hair, it is a glory to her" (1 Cor. 11:14-15).

Christian school administrators are called upon to function as the spiritual leaders of their schools along with a host of other duties. They must interpret such scriptures into standards of appearance that are, in their judgment, commensurate with the teachings of God's Word.

Most young people are reasonable individuals and will accept a sincere, honest explanation of why something is wrong if it can be demonstrated in God's Word. In general, Christian young people truly want to follow the Lord. And they will—if the spiritual guideposts around them are all saying the same thing. A problem many school principals have with enforcing dress codes and other school rules is that a few parents and even some pastors will not support them. This creates a crisis for young people who are doing their best to honor the Lord. I heard a principal say, "Some of the girls in my school save their short dresses and wear them on Sunday." This is a problem. Students have a tendency to gravitate to the road of least resistance. If the standards at home and church are not consistent with the school, the principal finds himself with his back against the wall and his rule book badly bent.

Another rule book bender is the 40-year-old majorette who glides into the school office to pay her child's tuition. The fact that she pays her child's tuition is not the problem. The problem is that her own standards of dress are not consistent with the standards of the school. She pays the school to uphold a standard that she is not willing to accept personally. Once again, the principal scratches his head and asks himself, "What's a principal to do?"

Even in this confusing time when the term *dress code* causes the average student to moan and the principal to groan, God's Word is still a "lamp unto our feet and a light unto our path" (Ps. 119:105). Paul reminds us, "Whatsoever ye do in word or deed, do all in the name of the Lord Jesus" (Col. 3:17).

The following is a quotation from the opening paragraphs of the dress code at Whittier Christian High School in California, written by the school's distinguished principal, Eugene Birdsall:

> A Christian institution has a unique responsibility in this area. Since we are judged largely by our appearance, we dare not be blind to the changing styles of the day and become so far "behind the times" and hopelessly "dated" that we repel the very ones who should be attracted by our Christian testimony. Nor do we dare offend by adopting styles and fads which are purposely suggestive and vulgar in their appeal or which are the unique trademark of segments of society decidedly ungodly in their influence. Our appearance then must be conservative so that we are not offensive, and in good taste so as to "adorn the Gospel" by our attractiveness.

If we take away the possibility
of failure, we take
away the need for God.

15

Should We Have Schools Without Failure?

Christian school educators place Christ and His holy Word at the very center of the school's curriculum and then try to study and teach everything they see through the eyes of God. They attempt to see the world and all of life, past, present, and future, as God sees it. To Christian school educators, if Christ is Lord of all, He is Lord of every minute detail of life including the everyday academic menu of the classroom. The educational purpose, the curriculum content, and the method of teaching must conform to biblical principles.

With this thought in mind, let's analyze the newest educational phenomenon, "schools without failure." You say, "What do you mean, 'schools without failure'?" It begins with Dr. William Glasser, a Los Angeles psychiatrist, the author of a new idea in education that is sweeping the country. His idea eliminates or minimizes those things in the educational process that might cause a youngster to experience failure. He would eliminate things such as textbooks, objective tests for evaluation, A-B-C-D-F grades, graded report cards, and punishment of any kind. In his book *Schools Without Failure* (Harper & Row, 1969) he says "Punishment does not work."

Dr. Glasser is a part of the new wave in education called "The Third Force" or "Humanistic Psychology." His program of education is based on "involvement, relevance, and thinking," which he assumes does not occur in the more traditional classroom. He would not agree with Cicero, who said, "He who is ignorant of what happened before his birth is always a child." Glasser (in *Schools Without Failure*) says of textbooks, "A better procedure would be to eliminate texts altogether and have each school district select books from the large variety of relevant, low-priced paperbacks now widely available." He would advocate such books as *West Side Story* and others.

Speaking of failure, in the same book, Glasser says, "Children, from the time they enter school, should be promised that they will not fail; to make this promise valid, they must not be labeled failures through failing grades."

As mentioned earlier, sometimes critics of Christian schools and colleges say that their students are unduly sheltered and are not adequately prepared for the cold realities of the "outside world." This, of course, is not generally true. But can you imagine the traumatic emotional experience of Glasser's students, who have never experienced failure in school, when they hit the cold realities of the outside world where failures are a part of everyday life?

Life is made up of both failure and success. Every youngster should have the educational opportunity that prepares him to cope with both ends of that emotional spectrum. An educational program that does not cope with both failure and success is "sheltering" in the first degree.

Dr. Glasser and his progressive education compatriots have the misguided idea that the lessons of failure are unimportant. Lessons in failure, however, are as important as lessons in success. In his book, Dr. Glasser records the results of an interesting survey of 342 graduates of Columbia University. "Those who had graduated from college with honors, who had won scholastic medals, who had been elected to Phi Beta Kappa, were more likely to be in the lower professional performance levels than in the top levels!" Dr. Glasser interprets this as another indication that grades are unimportant to education.

Perhaps a more realistic interpretation would be that brilliant students in school succeed so consistently that they never learn the lessons of failure in their educational experience. Consequently, they are not as well prepared for the workaday world as their less brilliant classmates who had to claw and scratch their way to the top.

Unfortunately, in Glasser's world of education, he cannot draw upon the counsel of the Apostle Paul who said to the Philippians, "I know both how to be abased, and I know how to abound; everywhere and in all things I am instructed both to abound and to suffer need. I can do all things through Christ which strengtheneth me" (4:12-13).

Public school educators by the thousands are drinking at the fountain of Glasser's ideas both at his Educational Training Center in Los Angeles and his seminars around the country. His experiences with youngsters and young people in the inner-city Watts area of Los Angeles and at the Ventura School for Girls of the California Youth Authority have caused him to conclude that these unsuccessful youngsters would have been successful had they enjoyed unlimited continuous success in school. His major point is that he wants youngsters to feel a greater degree of success. But how is a child to enjoy the thrill of success if there is no opportunity or even possibility of failure? Without the potential of failure there can be no sensation of success.

Christian school educators whom I know are guided by a biblical work ethic. Those who work are rewarded and those who do not work are not rewarded. Dr. Glasser would have considerable difficulty accepting the directive of the Apostle Paul to the Thessalonians, "This we commanded you, that if any would not work, neither should he eat." (2 Thes. 3:10). Dr. Glasser, it would appear, does not like the idea of anybody being left out—even those who do not work.

You say, "How do teachers in Christian schools handle youngsters who have not learned to perform at their best potential or who, because of their limitations, experience considerable failure?" Paul said, concerning those who will not work, "Count him not as an enemy, but admonish him as a brother" (2 Thes. 3:15). Christian schools may have their failures but the goal is not to treat them as enemies or even hopeless failures. Christian school students who encounter academic failure, or failure at home, or social failure, or even spiritual failure need to be encouraged to put their trust in God and to develop a continual dependence upon Him. In a Christian school, the negative experiences of failure often become the building blocks of success. Students are not sheltered from failure but they are exposed to the way out of failure by depending upon Christ, the eternal Source of victory for us all.

Turning failures into successes is the warp and woof of learning to walk with the Lord. Youngsters in Christian schools are inspired to believe God's Word, including such Scripture as "Trust in the Lord with all thine heart; and lean not unto thine own understanding" (Prov. 3:5); "Commit thy way unto the Lord; trust also in Him; and He shall bring it to pass" (Ps. 37:5); and the account of the 16-year-old King Uzziah of whom it was said, "As long as he sought the Lord, God made him to prosper" (2 Chron. 26:5). These, of course, are strange words to secularists in the field of education who have no One to reach up to in times of failure.

Should we have schools without failure? I don't believe the Lord would have it so. If we take away the possibility of failure, we take away the need for God. When we come to Christ for salvation, the very first requirement is to admit we are sinful failures and our only hope is our complete trust in Christ our Redeemer. From that moment on, our trust must be in God in every area of our lives including the day-to-day challenge of education.

If we keep Christ and His Word
at the center of our schools,
I see them as the brightest ray of
hope . . . for our country.

16

The Future
of Christian
Schools

Today's new Christian schools do not claim perfection. I would not leave that impression. Some are better staffed and equipped than others. But all that I know of are striving to excel in the area of education, with Christ and the Bible at the center of their teaching programs. Even the safe and sane public schools can hardly make that statement.

But what about the future of Christian school education? Will it continue to grow? Christian schools now represent the fastest growing educational movement in America. Will the present-day momentum—"The Christian School Explosion" or "The Protestant Boom"—continue? I am asked these questions many times in a variety of ways. My answer is always the same—yes! Quite frankly, if the Lord delays His coming, the current phenomenon of Christian school growth is only the beginning.

If we will keep Christ and His Word at the center of our schools, I see them as the brightest ray of hope—perhaps the only ray of hope—for our country. Someone has said, "The survival of democracy does not depend on the survival of common schools but on common values." The values Christian schools teach are vital to survival only because they are centered in the Word of God. Christian schools, as academic institutions, are not the answer. Christ and His Word *in* the Christian schools *is* the answer. The day the Christian school movement loses its commitment to God's Word will be the first day of its demise. If Christian school teachers and principals will remember that in Christian school education the word *Christian* comes before the word *school,* then this movement which is currently the talk of the country will turn the world upside down.

Martin Luther had unbelievably prophetic insight when he said: "I am much afraid that schools will prove to be the great gates of hell, unless they diligently labor in explaining the Holy Scriptures, engraving them in the hearts of youth. I advise no one to place his child where the Scriptures do not reign paramount. Every institution in which men are not unceasingly occupied with the Word of God must become corrupt."

I receive scores of letters from listeners to my radio program in California. One wrote a startling letter to me giving an example of a "Christian" school where the spiritual light has gone out. Here, in part, is her letter:

> I caught your program on KHOF radio last Wednesday as I was on my way to an employment agency. It must have been God's plan for me to tune in when I did.

For the past two years, I have been teaching in a "liberal Protestant church school" here in the Los Angeles area. In recent weeks, the children have become loud, obscene, violent, and lewd. When I decided to bring the Bible into the classroom and read Bible stories during the lunch hour to bring a moral and loving atmosphere on campus, I was informed that parents chose our school because the school's leaders have promised they would not permit any religious instruction. We go to chapel each morning, recite the Lord's Prayer and a nonoffending children's prayer, sing a hymn, and leave for class.

To be sure I understood the directive, the school board president met personally with me and spelled it out. If I ever mentioned God, Jesus Christ, or the Bible, or left my religious pictures on my bulletin board, I would be fired. I felt as though this was a scene from the Dark Ages. I am most unhappy in this situation and feel most uncomfortable when children bring in their Bible stories and continue to ask questions about Jesus and God and I am not permitted to satisfy their interest of the moment. It is a certainty that I will not be given another contract.

I need your help, for I honestly want to teach in a Christian school and prefer this to taking just any job. Could you assist me in finding a position?

We did, indeed, assist her in finding a teaching position in a *Christian* school. I met her later at the CACS statewide teachers convention in Fresno, Calif. She was happy in her ministry as a teacher in a school where the lordship of Christ is honored.

Her letter truly solemnized me. It helped me realize that spiritual depravity is not limited to secular schools. It gave me a descriptive picture of what can happen to a Christian school where the Word of God is no longer held in esteem above every other book.

I suppose Harvard, Yale, and Columbia Universities are the classic examples of schools that were once Christian, but have long since lost their commitment to promoting the Gospel of Jesus Christ. Harvard, Yale, and Columbia were once bastions of evangelical fervor. Harvard University, founded in 1636, just 16 years after the pilgrims landed at Plymouth Rock, was named after John Harvard, a flaming evangelist. A major purpose of the early colleges was to train young men for the ministry. There is not the slightest pretense now among those Ivy League colleges of identifying with their original Christ-centered purposes.

As we look at the history of religious educational institutions at all levels, it seems that spiritual decline is inevitable. But I am convinced that it does not have to happen.

Some years ago Dr. Roy Lowrie asked veteran Christian school pioneer Dr. Mark Fakkema, "What is your first bit of advice to Christian school educators today?"

He replied, "Keep Christian schools *Christian!*"

I believe, with God's help, that is being done. There is more focus on the centrality of Christ and His Word in Christian schools today than there was 10 years ago. As Christian school educators warm up to the task and prepare to "contend for the faith," they are being drawn to a position of dependence upon the Lord.

I am convinced that parents who send their youngsters to Christian schools today are motivated for spiritual reasons more so than they were a few years ago. And therein lies a major key to keeping Christian schools Christian. Christian schools can best serve parents who want more than mechanical academics for their children. Any quality school can provide academics. Christian school educators are looking for parents who feel strongly, as they do, about inspiring young people to life-long commitments to Christ and to Christian principles. They are looking for parents who will stand with them in their emphasis on love of country, respect for parental and civil authority, and loyalty to church and to Christian friendships. Christian schools, as I know them, are committed to quality academic programs that have Christ at the center. The Apostle Paul said, speaking of Christ, "That in all things He might have the pre-eminence" (Col. 1: 18). This is the very heart of a vibrant future for Christian schools.

Someone asked me, "What will happen to Christian schools if prayers are reinstated in public schools, if there is a decline in the use of drugs by students, and there is a general return to 'normalcy' in public education?"

First of all, if such a complete turnabout were to occur, to my knowledge, ours would be the first civilization in history to undergo a self-imposed meta-morphic redemptive turnaround. Civilizations of man have a consistent record of downward trends.

Second, secular education is so completely peopled and supported by the liberal community, only the wildest dreamer could predict a return to "normalcy."

Third, and most important, the Christian school movement is God's school system. He did not bring it into being to have it suddenly disappear. The Christian community is now sensitive to its value. Christians are supporting Christian schools in ever growing number. This is God's time for Christian education.

In the fall, winter, and spring, cold rain is a major feature of Oregon, my home state. This brings many things, including an abundance of small green frogs. These are hardy little creatures. I used to carry them around in my pocket. It is amazing how they could survive in there with my typical boy's pocket filled with "pretty" rocks, pocket knife, nails, marbles, and other valuables.

Occasionally a frog would "accidentally" be in my pocket as I went into class at school. Sometimes when the lessons got a little boring for me, which occurred quite often, I tried to attract the attention of the girls by taking my frog out of my pocket. I held the frog firmly in my hand and squeezed him a little bit to make his eyes bug out. That nearly always got their attention. Sometimes, however, I overdid it, and the alarm registered by the girls was noticed by the teacher. Big trouble for me, in the form of a perceptive teacher, came marching right down the aisle to my desk. Most of the time the teacher was not fast enough to catch me before I quickly unbuttoned my shirt and popped my green frog inside. As I unloaded my pockets on the desk top for the teacher, I always tried to look as mystified as possible about the whole commotion. After things were back to normal, my frog friend would start moving around under my shirt along the top of my belt. Every so often he would jump, which caused my shirt to take on strange movements. This, too, created a sensation with the girls but never great enough to bring the teacher back to my desk.

I learned a lot about frogs. I do not recommend you do this, but I learned, for example, that you can take a frog and drop him in a pan of very hot water. He will immediately react to the high temperature, and if the pan is shallow enough, he will hop out and over the side. You can take that same frog, however, or perhaps you should use a second frog, and drop him in a pan of cold water. Light a fire under the pan and heat the water gradually until it is very hot. The frog will sit there placidly blinking his eyes at you as the pan of water gets hotter and hotter. He just sits there and assimilates the heat. He will actually allow the hot water to destroy him not knowing the temperature around him is rising.

I mention this because our human conscience is a bit like the frog in the pan of water. The temperature around us is rising and many Christians are not responding. If all of the present-day evidence of man's depravity had come upon us at one time, we, in typical American fashion, would have responded. We would have fought back. We would have, like all good men, come to the aid of our country.

But what we now see as increasing corruption and moral decay in government, in education, and in industry has come at us in the form of one small headline at a time, day after day. If we do not respond soon, we, like the frog, will casually blink our eyes once too often in our pan of rising temperature and we, the American nation, will be gone.

But it does not have to happen! If those Americans who still have enough spiritual perception to respond to danger signals will listen to the wisdom of an ancient Hebrew proverb, "Train up a child in the way he should go and when he is old he will not depart from it" (Prov. 22:6), then there is hope for us and the generations to follow.